TRAGEDY TURNED UPSIDE DOWN

GOD'S SUPREME GOODNESS IN OUR DARKEST TIMES

Cindy Schmidler

LUCIDBOOKS

Tragedy Turned Upside Down
God's Supreme Goodness in Our Darkest Times

Copyright © 2020 by Cindy Schmidler

Published by Lucid Books in Houston, TX
www.LucidBooksPublishing.com

ISBN: 978-1-63296-800-5
eISBN: 978-1-63296-383-3

Special Sales: Most Lucid Books titles are available in special quantity discounts. Custom imprinting or excerpting can also be done to fit special needs. Contact Lucid Books at Info@LucidBooksPublishing.com.

"I am so grateful for Cindy Schmidler—her life, her passion, her love for God, and her love for others. She has been a true blessing in my life and in my family's lives. I am thrilled that Cindy decided to share her life story of cancer, brokenness, hope, and redemption. I truly believe this is a book that will inspire any and all who read it and will preserve them in the midst of life's challenges and hold them to the one who ultimately holds our lives and writes our stories for our good and for his glory. The beauty the reader will find in the midst of the ashes will help to remind them that the battles we face won't ever have the final word because God has already drawn for his children the ultimate victory."

—Orlando Cabrera,
Lead Campus Pastor, Summit Church, Fort Myers, Florida

"*Tragedy Turned Upside Down* is a strange title unless you understand that God will use anything to bring us to a saving faith. Cindy Schmidler is a living testimony of God's grace. Cindy and her husband, John, are truly inspirational. If you need real hope, the kind that doesn't depend on circumstance, if you are in a deep valley and need to know God is still good, this book is a must-read. May it bless you, and may God meet you between the pages as scripture comes alive through this heartfelt story."

—Garrett Higbee,
Director of Pastoral Care, Great Commission Collective
Founding Board Member, Biblical Counseling Coalition
President, Twelve Stones Ministries

"Suffering rarely knocks. It crashes life's party, uninvited, sometimes refusing to leave. It's like a squatter, this suffering—inhabiting one's body and mind with the intention of laying claim. Where is God when suffering confuses all your categories, when cancer sets up camp for a long stay?

Cindy gets it. And it's not because she's read about suffering or spoken with experts on cancer. Cindy's been there. She's known the life-sapping, bone-wearying fatigue of chemo and battled in the darkness.

But don't make the mistake of thinking that this book is simply about surviving cancer. This book is about Jesus. It's about the difference he makes when suffering arrives unannounced. It's about the promises of God and how they stir faith, inspire courage, and produce in us the resilience to face another day.

Let Cindy's journey guide your own. Let her point the way so that you, too, can discover that Jesus not only transforms us through suffering, but he is enough."

—Dave Harvey,
Author, *I Still Do* and *When Sinners Say "I Do"*
President, Great Commission Collective

"I met Cindy Schmidler one morning when I delivered books to the Bible study she was teaching. It was one of those God-connecting-the-dots moments. Since then, my wife and I have been blessed as we have watched and participated in Cindy's passion to tell others about her love for Jesus.

Her story is like Paul's experience on the road to Damascus except Cindy met Jesus on the road to cancer. It was life-changing—an eternal, life-changing experience and a story you'll want to hear."

—Michael Belk,
Photographer and Author, *Journeys with the Messiah*

"It is with much pleasure that I highly recommend Cindy Schmidler's book, *Tragedy Turned Upside Down*. From the first page, the book grabbed my attention, and it kept me interested until the very end. Not only did it hold my interest, but it made me want to talk about it with others—whoever would listen, in fact. As I read, it made me hunger and thirst for more of Jesus—not more of Cindy but more of Jesus. It made me feel hopeful.

The book touches on things that frankly terrify me, but it gave me hope that the same God who was with Cindy in her suffering would also equip me to be able to handle victoriously whatever suffering I would face. Each of us has a desire to be found faithful no matter what our circumstances. Cindy tells her personal story of the faithfulness of God to her, from ashes to beauty, in her day-to-day journey through her cancer diagnosis.

The book points to the sweet fact that intimacy with Jesus is our deepest need and our greatest treasure."

—Desiree Mortensen,
Women's Ministry Leader and Speaker

To my person, my bff, John. You never wavered in the thickest refuse of our mud, enabling me to press on with all God's power in me. You're the real hero of my story. I couldn't have done it without you. The best part: growing old and wrinkly together, loving God and each other more every day.

To my dearest son, Adam. You are the brightest light in my world. Your demonstration of man-strength and no-holds-barred love in my cancer, forsaking friends and fun, showed me the substantial person you have become (I've always known it). I love you more than the sand on the seashore.

Table of Contents

Foreword

I am convinced that we are all looking for stories that give us hope, that help us know we are not alone in the issues we struggle with and the answers we are searching for. I believe there is a God who sees us, knows what we need, and will hear and answer us when we pray. Cindy's life is filled with such stories as she recounts them in her marvelous, hope-infused book. When confronted with a life-threatening cancer diagnosis at the young age of 23, she was among the many who desperately look for hope, even as she feared she was dying. This desperation led her to search for answers about God and how she could know what would happen if she were to die. The journey of her life as she discovered those answers and came to know the God who would faithfully walk with her through illness, seasons of uncertainty, and painful times of grief and loss, even as he provided for her in her deepest longings, is what you hold in your hands.

I have known Cindy for more than 20 years. It has been a gift in many ways to be her friend through many seasons of life. My faith is stronger because of how I have seen the Lord work in her life. I have watched in more ways than I can count how the Lord has consistently used her, her faith, and the intimacy she has with him to bless, encourage, and lead many to Jesus. Cindy's experiences with cancer, infertility, and unimaginable loss have made her and her husband, John, compassionate, faith-filled, and merciful guides for others who are struggling with similar experiences and are suffering, hopeless, and confused.

Even as I write this foreword, I am moved with emotion recalling how Cindy and John showed up at our bedside in the hospital 11 years ago when my husband, Newt, was diagnosed with lymphoma after a three-week roller coaster of uncertainty, tests, and biopsies. We will never forget their kindness, compassion, wise understanding, and powerful prayers for us, even as they pointed us to Jesus and his perfect and timely Word—exactly what we needed at that moment. Because they, too, had experienced the comfort of God during cancer, they were able to comfort and minister to us with the comfort they had received. And two years later, after Newt's healing, we were able to be there for them, doing the same and reminding them of God's Word for them when Cindy faced another cancer challenge.

Through all that Cindy has experienced, God has been by her side, hearing her prayers, revealing himself to her, and growing her into a woman who has stewarded her pain well by allowing it to mature her in wisdom, faith, and intimacy with the one who has walked with her through it all. Over the years, Cindy has ministered to hundreds of women through her Bible studies, counseling ministry, and friendships. Her ministry flows out of what the Lord has taught her as she has learned to hear, depend on, and trust him through the storms and trials of her life. I have been privileged to be in Bible study and prayer groups with her, and I have experienced her love and bold, courageous, and unashamed faith for the Lord Jesus Christ as she bears witness to him and his Word for us all.

The book you hold in your hand is a treasure. The hand and kindness of God in providing, rescuing, and revealing himself to Cindy is real and unmistakable. I am confident that as you read this book, you, too, will see God in and through her story. After all, it is his story that he has written for her, that all who would hear it would witness his faithfulness and goodness to his children who put their hope in him.

—**Susan Crenshaw,**
Wife of the President of Young Life
Colorado Springs, Colorado

Introduction

W hat if today could be blue skies, smooth sailing, and warm winds on our backs. The truth is that most days are anything but that. Every day is a fight for abundant, breathtaking exhilaration, right?

I wrote because of God's promptings—*Tell of my wonderful deeds, my inexhaustible treasures, my all-knowing, all-enabling purpose*—and that's where our guts to endure lie.

When life has bankrupted us and we feel desperately raw, when we've been dealt an unfair hand, when our emotions have spilled onto our sleeves, that's when God's supreme abilities for our good should shine. We need the ability to focus on what is actually and purposefully going on behind closed doors.

The Lord tells us that his ways are high and heavenly (Isa. 55:8–11). We need God's warming blanket of comfort and support to truly relieve our level-10 pain.

This book provides a vital understanding of God when it comes to our severest suffering. It reveals *his* commanding position in our every circumstance and *his* complete control and goodness in handling our worst tragedies. It's how God's plan *was* my cancer. It's how God had preplanned our son's sickness for his good and perfectly fixed purpose, just like Lazarus in John 11:4.

This plan of his—such a difficult one—had many superior and truly remarkable purposes. As I began to get a glimpse into his

1

preplanning of my calamity, it changed everything for me. Hope—actual, authentic hope—began rising. My first sense of optimism flowed through my crusty, hard, nonliving, believing veins.

The thought—a true, right thought—is that he planned it; therefore, it's exceptional and has his supreme objective in it. Wow! Now that's inspiring!

Today as I'm writing to you, God has worked in a dear friend's life. Mary, who is 60-something, recently lost her soul mate, the love of her life, and now God has provided her another wonderful man. She's thinking that this is completely, utterly impossible—this feeling of such giddiness, lighthearted excitement over someone other than her now-dead soul mate. Ridiculous, right? Her emotions are running rampant; it's wildly absurd. All those dark, gruesome hospital days with her dying love, and now she's fallen off her rocker, unhinged and delirious. But God!

> *The righteous cry out, and the LORD hears them;*
> *he delivers them from all their troubles.*
> *The LORD is close to the brokenhearted*
> *and saves those who are crushed in spirit.*
>
> *The righteous person may have many troubles,*
> *but the LORD delivers him from them all.*
>
> —Ps. 34:17–19

> *Many, LORD my God,*
> *are the wonders you have done,*
> *the things you planned for us.*
>
> —Ps. 40:5

Come and join me in the pages of this book where God has written my story and where true hope rises.

CHAPTER ONE

Breathe, Cindy, Breathe

Finally, all my plans were crystallizing, and my dreams were coming alive right before my eyes. I was only 23 and married to the love of my life, John, who, in my opinion, is better than thick, gooey french toast dipped in buttery pecan syrup. Oh, how I love that gooey toast! He's the greatest, most handsome, most gregarious life of the party; he's the smartest, most caring guy on the planet, and he adores *me*.

Most men I'd dated seemed to care more about themselves and their gadgets—you know, man stuff like cars, technology, devices—than relationships like we girls live for. But John had a depth and sensitivity I hadn't seen before. He seemed to clearly understand the world around him. It was so unusual, so refreshing. I felt like a girl with a heavenly, scrumptious, warm chocolate lava cake in front of her and a fork in hand. Could this moment last forever? How much more fortunate could one person be? I was so elated, so proud to call this kind, handsome man my husband.

I will plan a beautiful, enchanting evening, I thought. *That will be the perfect diversion.* Our apartment, cozy as it was, could feel a little claustrophobic by the end of the day, and with a weather-breaking evening ahead, this warm night was my perfect escape. The long, gray winter had finally drawn back its heavy mantle, and life was beginning to blossom. I longed for the aroma of summer in the flowers and fresh-cut grass. I wanted to grab hold of it with all my gusto—seize the evening, get freedom from my reality. *Maybe we could do some activity under the night sky*, I thought. We could invite Mitch, Tami, Steve, and Michelle for dinner—a festive evening under the stars, that's what I'll do. *The more guests the merrier*, I thought. Cajun-style shrimp pasta with a fresh Mediterranean salad for dinner sounds delicious. I could smell the spicy Cajun already. *Maybe that new Rachael Ray recipe I saw on TV yesterday would be good.* Now, that sounds like a terrific plan, if I do say so myself. It would be a delightful, exhilarating night.

This is the fairy-tale night I dreamed of, the one I deserved, I tried to tell myself with everything in me. But truth be told, in a moment, it all fell apart. I could no longer feel the warm breeze floating across my cheeks or see the night sky shining with a million twinkling lights.

My heart plummeted. I slumped down to the kitchen floor, feeling my heart pounding outside my chest. "I have some bad news. There's a grapefruit-sized tumor wrapped around your heart and lungs."

That news I had heard days earlier leaked back into my brain, hijacking my complete denial. It was a bright neon sign squishing in every crevice I'd tried to empty in my mind, saying, "You are dying."

What? What did the doctor just say? A tumor? But I was 23. Those words were for hospice rooms, elderly bedsides, cancer wings, and dark, dramatic movies about other people's terrible misfortunes— not mine. Not my perfect life. *Breathe, Cindy, breathe!* I told my lungs to breathe, but they were frozen. My body shook erratically, my face felt flushed, and my blood boiled. Panic had overtaken me.

How could this be? The world was my oyster—a peaceful, wonderful, twinkling, light summer ahead. Now I was faced with what? Possibly death? Was I dying? My legs felt tingly, numb. I couldn't walk. Was death taking me now? Was I dying this minute, right now? *Someone, please help me*, my heart cried.

"Dr. Small." My voice was weak. "Could I die?"

"I'm sorry, Cindy. I don't know."

How could she not know?

This was the brick that shattered my rosy window.

What was I thinking, trying to deny my reality? Children pretend.

I had to excuse myself from that starry night, my perfectly planned evening that ended in a spatter because it wasn't my reality.

The Early Years

When I was a young girl, my mom and dad spent most days at the hospital with my younger brother, Jeff, who was born without an esophagus. By the time he was two, he already had seven major operations under his belt. I spent a lot of time with Nana, my grandma who lived upstairs in our duplex.

I had two dolls as tall as I was, a blonde and a brunette. Every day we had a tea party in Nana's apartment.

"Cindy, let me get the tea," Nana would say. It was just water in my play tea set. She served me chunks of butter and tablespoons of sugar. She must have taken Mary Poppins's spoonful of sugar a little too literally.

Nana always had a smiling disposition. I knew everything was going to be okay when she was around. When I grew older, I learned that her husband, my grandfather, had passed away suddenly of a massive heart attack when my mom was just five. Nana then went to work to provide for Mom and Aunt Barb. Even at such a young age, I could tell something was different about Nana. I think she always knew God was with her, taking care of her, watching her comings and goings. Could her faith, her lighthearted trust, have permeated me as an adolescent?

Sometimes Mom and Dad sneaked me up the hospital elevator to see Jeff. Since I was only four, I wasn't allowed on his floor. We'd meet in the elevator and giggle at the tubes coming out of his body. I'd want to push him around on the wheelchair and climb onto the seat to be next to him. When he did come home from the hospital, Mom fed him all his meals through a tube in his stomach. This was all normal life for me then, and I wonder if God was preparing me for what would come next by watching my brother.

When Jeff was two years old, the surgeons made a makeshift esophagus from his intestines. That was 55 years ago as of the time of this writing, and he still has his substitute esophagus. He lives a very active, athletic life. Nana said it was a miracle. She was a big churchgoer and Bible-reader. I would see her in her bedroom, sitting in her corner recliner, saying her rosary, and reading her Bible. Mom went to church once in a while, but Dad never did.

On Sundays, Nana would come downstairs and get me ready so she could take me to church. She was instilling in me those valuable principals that God cares for us. I always wondered why she spent so much time in that bedroom chair talking with God. Looking back, I understand. We never missed a Sunday, and while church was important to Nana, for me it was just a fun day out. I loved riding the bus there and back with her. Was God preparing me for my future? I say yes, absolutely, because all these moments were written in his book (Ps. 139).

As I got a little older, I'd often walk to the bluffs and climb down to the beach at Lake Michigan to meet up with my friends. Together, we would search for lost treasure. Quarters, dimes, nickels—we dug deep in the sand and found dollars in change. We couldn't wait to see one another. We spent every summer at our little yacht club, sailing and swimming. In the winter, we'd skate and sled. My life revolved around who was going to bring the toboggan and whose parents were driving us to the hill.

We lived life fully. Our sledding hill was dangerously high. I remember climbing to the top, looking down, and thinking, *I don't want to do this. It's too steep. It's so high! What a thrill! I'm so afraid but so excited.* We would pile up on our rickety sleds, and someone would push us before we were ready. Down we'd fly at what felt like 100 miles per hour. It was called Suicide Hill for a reason, and although someone was always getting hurt, we decided the injuries were worth it. My childhood was adventuresome, and because I felt secure to adventure out, God was showing me what influence my family atmosphere had on preparing me for when cancer would knock at my door. Security in family enabled me to connect to my heavenly Father in my greatest time of need.

Dinner was always a priority at our house. I couldn't wait for Mom's delicious homemade pork roast with mashed potatoes smothered in gravy. Her gravy was the best. Then it was off to the basement to help with one of Dad's many ongoing projects. He put us to work sanding wood or painting fiberglass on molds of boats he was building. He was always making something. As a master builder, he could build anything—houses, boats, and little sailboat racers for Jeff and me. We'd hop in his blue-and-white, tail-finned Chrysler to go get nails. I sat right next to him, drowning in the white leather bench seat, jibber-jabbering all the way to the hardware store where he'd stare at aisles of nails for what seemed like hours. Dad loved nails.

I was learning necessary attributes of a father's love, care, and security during those years, things I know, today, have helped me trust my heavenly Father. To this day, the smell of freshly cut wood reminds me of Dad's tender care.

My high school was right across the street from Lake Michigan. I immediately gravitated to the nonathletic, popular kids. This proved to be a stumbling block and caused me much heartache in my high school years as I navigated through the rough and tumble. By the time I started college, I got my head on the straight and narrow road. Science and animals had become my first love, and I majored in zoology. What can you do with a zoology degree, anyway? It wasn't the greatest degree for a successful career.

I met John at college, and he instantly became the love of my life. He was the one. John was in the engineering program, and

I was in the sciences, so it's hardly a surprise that we met in the library. Don't kid yourself, though; we definitely loved our parties. We became inseparable, practically joined at the hip. John was smart, handsome, and fun to be around. I was impressed with his brilliance and flattered by his admiration of me. Of course, it was all about me. He proposed, and eight months later we had a large, big-band wedding. Then we were off to the Caribbean for a traditional honeymoon. Perfect husband, perfect life.

Leaving home and friends for Indianapolis after we were married was extremely hard. It was my first experience away from home, and I had cried all the way there. I didn't know a single person in that flat city in the middle of midwestern farm country. John's company had transferred him there, but I had nothing to do. For my sanity, I decided to look at living in this new city as an adventure.

We moved to a large apartment complex on the west side of Indianapolis, a landlocked city. The thought of Indianapolis—a city without any large bodies of water—was devastating to me. Where was I going to sail, swim, and sun? Soon we met Janet and Cathy who lived on the first floor of our building, and then Tami and Mitch on the second floor, Michelle who lived alone, and Kevin and Steve who also lived on the first floor. Before long, we had all become good friends. We barbecued, watched *Dallas* on TV, and thankfully, sailed and swam in our little community lake. Of course, the single guys were after the single girls. Kevin ended up marrying Michelle, and they had three children.

That fall, I developed a severe cold that made my whole body ache. I was so stuffed up that I couldn't breathe through my nose, and my throat was burning with raw pain. It went on and on, leaving me miserably cranky and exhausted. Why wasn't I getting better? I was so frustrated, sick, and tired of being sick.

John urged me to go to the doctor and get some antibiotics, but seeing a doctor for a cold felt crazy to me. To get him to stop nagging me, I made an appointment with a local doctor and called Janice to come with me. She was available, so I picked her up, and we made the short, 10-minute trip. I have no idea why I asked her to come along, but I did. She was just an acquaintance, not a friend.

I fussed all the way there. Why in the world was I doing this? It's ridiculous to go to the doctor for a cold. Pulling into a parking spot, my chest seized, and I went into a coughing fit, reminding my brain why I was there. As I got out of the car, my legs felt like lead weights. I had to drag myself into the brownstone building. Janice and I stepped into the elevator with four others. Room 202 on the second floor was to the right as we exited the elevator.

I opened the office door to a large waiting room full of people— sick, coughing, sneezing, blowing their noses. I had never seen so many red-eyed, drippy-nosed people in one room. Yuck! Luckily, a nurse quickly called me into a room.

"Cindy?" the nurse shouted across the crowded room.

"Right here." I left my poor neighbor in that virus-filled room. Feeling guilty but too tired to care, I followed the nurse to my exam room, making chit-chat niceties on the way.

"Cindy, why are you here today?" the nurse asked.

"I have a very severe cold that will not go away."

"Please undress waist up, and put this gown on, front side open."

I waited for what felt like an eternity and looked for something to occupy myself, but there were only medical pamphlets and brochures. Not interested. The last thing I needed was to work myself up about medical diseases. The only pictures on the wall were the doctor's credentials—you know, the I-graduated-from-Stanford-with-blah-blah-blah certificates.

I got up on the table, thinking I'd be ready when the doctor came in and get it over faster. I could hear her in the hall finishing up with a young woman. A tall, slender woman walked in.

"I'm Dr. Small," she said, and shook my hand. "So you're here because you have a respiratory ailment."

"Yes. My husband insisted I come."

After I gave her my cold symptoms—bad congestion, cough, fever, chills, sweats at night, tired all the time, nagging sore throat—she said, "I'm sure you have this virus going around, but I would like to x-ray your chest to make sure it's not pneumonia. I had a patient yesterday with pneumonia, so I'd like to take that precaution."

"Okay. Do whatever you need to do."

Thankfully, they were a one-stop shop, and the X-ray room was on the first floor. The nurse took me to the lab where I waited. I had never had an X-ray before, so this was all new to me. The technician asked me to lean in and press against a panel on her machine. "Put your hands over your head, breathe in as much air into your lungs as you possibly can, and hold it," she said. About four seconds later, she said I could breathe. This happened a couple of times, and then I was finished and escorted back to my exam room where I waited again for the results. My poor neighbor was still in that petri dish of a waiting room. This was taking much longer than I had planned. It was so absurd, so preposterous for a cold. I hoped they had better entertainment out there for Janice, maybe some food or decorating magazines.

As I sat there alone with my thoughts, the small room began to close in on me. It was tattered and worn, and probably thousands had passed through with different ailments. The dull, yellow paint faded into the drywall. The pictures must have been from the '50s—countryside typical of Indiana farm country.

Time stood still, and after what felt like an hour had passed, my head was pounding, and I just wanted to go home. What in the world could take so long? *I should open the door because clearly they have forgotten me*, I thought. *I should call for the nurse. How embarrassing in my gown opened in the front.* Finally, the doctor stepped in with results in her hand. "Well, you do not have pneumonia, but I have found a mass in your chest."

She said the words *a mass in your chest* so casually.

What? I was beginning to melt down, literally disintegrate. *Mass* sounded so big and so cancerous. So deadly! How had I gone from never having gone to a doctor to having an image of my chest to now having a mass in my chest?

"How large is it?" I asked.

"Fifteen centimeters, or about the size of a deluxe grapefruit," she answered.

I knew what a deluxe grapefruit looked like—*big*.

My heart pounded as if it were coming out of my chest. I felt light-headed, as if any second I was going to pass out. Terror was setting in. I felt hysterical; my stomach was flipping as I searched the four walls for something to throw up in. Holding it back, I tried to understand what she was telling me.

"Could I die?" I asked. "Am I dying right now? What is it?"

"I really cannot tell you until we do a CAT scan ASAP," she said.

She couldn't tell me what it was or if I was dying.

"I'm so sorry," were her parting words.

I was so astonished I couldn't think of anything else to ask her. My body had started trembling. I couldn't breathe from the panic. My heart was pounding so hard it felt like it would burst out of my chest wall. I left the exam room and met Janice in the waiting room. I really didn't know her very well—definitely not well enough to share my grapefruit tumor and possible death with her. But what was I to do? This was too much for me to keep in, so I blurted out what the doctor had told me, describing the mass the size of a deluxe grapefruit in my chest.

Since I was in pieces, she offered to drive us home. In the meantime, the doctor scheduled a CAT scan appointment. I would have to wait to see if this mass was killing me. Of course, it was killing me; it was wrapped around my heart and lungs. The knowledge became my all-consuming mantra—a massive tumor wrapped inside my chest was killing me. It dawned on me how important it was that I'd had someone with me that day and that John had prompted me to go in the first place. Come to find out, God knew. He had been orchestrating these appointments all along. He says to "give thanks in all circumstances; for this is God's will for you" (1 Thess. 5:18).

When we got back to our apartment complex, I called John at work. What would I tell him? *Oh, honey, I have a grapefruit-sized tumor in my chest, and I'm probably going to die.* I thought about it and decided I would talk with his assistant, whom I loved, an older gal and wiser than myself. I thought it would be easier to spill my guts to her than the love of my life.

I picked up the phone and, with my heart pounding, waited for her to answer. "Hello, Joyce speaking." It was her. Now it was time to tell someone the most horrible news I'd ever been given.

"Joyce, I have a mass the size of a grapefruit in my chest. The doctor does not know if I'll die; they just don't know anything. Could you get John to come home right away and not scare him?"

What a tall order for an assistant—surely not in her job description. I can't even imagine what she was thinking.

I have no idea what she actually said to him, but when he walked through the door, I ran to him and broke down, explaining everything through my sobs. He asked many unanswerable questions, consoling me as he queried me. The seriousness of my explanation was beginning to set in, and John grew quiet. The news was unimaginable to us, surreal, not even in our thought process. We were simply too young for this kind of report. We were panic-stricken with way too many questions and no answers. We had no experience with health crises, and we had no family in Indianapolis to turn to.

How could we tell our parents who lived five hours away and were just getting used to us being married less than a year and living in another state? It seemed too delicate to share over the phone, so we quickly packed our overnight bags, jumped in the car, and started driving the five hours to Milwaukee, Wisconsin. It was getting late, and both of us were frazzled and dog-tired.

An hour into our trip, I felt my legs going numb. I knew I was dying.

"I don't think I can make this drive," I told John. "I don't think I can go any farther. What if I'm dying?"

Poor John was scared to death, too. Was my mind playing tricks? How could I know? How could anyone know? There were too many questions whirling around and no answers to be found. John turned the car around and raced home to call the doctor. When the physician on call answered (of course, it was after hours—it's always after hours), I explained that my legs were going numb.

"Am I dying?" I asked her.

"I do not know," she said. "I cannot tell you." *How could no one answer this most important question?* She offered to prescribe tranquilizers to calm me down. *What would calm me down are some answers.*

Death terrified me. What would it feel like? Was it painful? I felt so lonely. John was right next to me, but I couldn't take him with me in death. It's a solo event. *Honey, please hurry with those tranquilizers; my mind is relentlessly a chaotic mess.* And we still needed to tell our parents. Since it was pitch-dark by then, we decided to call them. How do you begin that conversation? I could minimize the story, leave out the wrapped-around-my-heart-and-lungs detail and call it a nodule that needs to be removed. That sounded less terrifying.

My fingers punched in my parents' number, and the ringing was deafening to my ears. "Mom? How are you?"

"I'm good," she answered. "It's a little late for you to be calling. Everything okay?" Moms know things.

"I'm fine. Can you put Dad on?"

"Hi, honey." Dad came on. "How are you?"

"I'm good, but I have to have a little surgery."

"What kind of surgery?"

I told them the doctor had found a small nodule in my chest, so she wants to remove it. I did my best to be calm and confident. After all, their questions had no answers because I had no answers. They backed off and decided to wait for test results from the CAT scan. John did the same thing with his parents.

It worked; they believed us. Why wouldn't they when we made it sound like a little blister? It was probably more of a lie than factual truth, but it was so hard living so far away with this horrible news. We would have to wait for tests anyway, so why worry them?

Meanwhile, I was drowning in tranquilizers, terrified of dying. I had to wait a full week for the CAT scan. Shortly after the scan, the result came in, showing that the tumor had wrapped itself around my heart and lungs, just as my doctor had originally told me. The doctor on the phone said it had made a home in there. Although he believed it was benign, he couldn't know for sure until he went in to remove it.

Wow! Were we thrilled that they didn't think it was cancerous! After a week of stressful waiting and not knowing, I don't have words to explain how completely elated John and I were to think it wasn't cancer. A renowned specialist in heart transplants was planning to saw open my breastbone, put me on a heart and lung machine, and then peel the tumor off like peeling an orange. At least that was how he explained the procedure to us.

While waiting for my surgery, I went to our community pool with a friend who just happened to be reading a *Time* magazine. In the magazine was an article detailing Hodgkin's disease, a cancer of the lymph nodes. As she read the article aloud to me, I went pale. I had every symptom she read. Had my mind started playing tricks again? One symptom of Hodgkin's disease is intense itching of the skin. Six months earlier, I had been to a dermatologist for my itchy skin. I had become so itchy that I couldn't sleep at night. I had thought I was allergic to my clothes. Another symptom was night sweats. I had often sweat through my clothes and gotten into the habit of changing my clothes nightly, thinking it was just too hot in the apartment.

I hurried home to our apartment and called my heart surgeon, whom I had not met yet, and made an appointment to see him. When I met with him, he appeared to be a very nice man, calming and confident. After I told him about the *Time* magazine article on

Hodgkin's disease and all the symptoms I was having, he reassured me that my tumor was probably benign and that he was going to keep with the plan of peeling it away like an orange.

"People with cancer have a look about them," he said, "and you don't look like you have cancer." That sounded good to me. Surely these physicians know about this stuff.

I entered the hospital the night before surgery to have the necessary prep work done before the procedure the next morning. The hospital was very old, a sturdy and stately brick-and-mortar building. I had a large room with tall ceilings like older homes have, and everything was light beige and shiny—all so typical of that type of building. On the wall in my room was an old-fashioned, large-numbered round clock, white with black numbers like the kind in elementary schools. It tick-tocked at what seemed like 10 decibels. I have never in my life heard a clock more deafening. Clocks aren't supposed to make noise. *Someone kill it, please.* I was going insane in that retro-furnished, too-large-for-comfort room. Between waiting for surgery, thinking about what they were going to do to me tomorrow, and the ticking clock, I was going mad.

My entire family was present. The first order of events before surgery was a very large female nurse coming into my room to give me an enema. *No thank you. No way,* I thought. *Old people get enemas, not 23-year-olds.* But the nurse told me to turn on my side. *Why couldn't they have drugged me up tonight so I wouldn't know what's going on? Here I am in a hospital waiting for major surgery. Growing up, we rarely even went to a doctor's office, only if we had a bad cut that needed stitches or had a broken bone.*

I had nothing to hang on to—no religion, no faith—and I was scared to death. I wished that Grandma's lighthearted countenance would radiate in me. I thought of her peace and her faith that everything was always going to be okay. Oh, how I wished I had her confidence, wished I knew the things she knew about God. I wished I believed like she believed. She was sure and certain in her faith.

A friend came to visit me that lonely night in the hospital. She went on and on about her dress shopping during the day. "Cindy, I found this great black dress, no sleeves, fitted with a small ruffle at the bottom. So classy yet trendy. I can't wait to wear it to Brad's office birthday party."

My ears were burning from the noise of her frivolous voice. Did she not know that I just had my first enema? In her defense, what do you say to your 23-year-old friend in the prime of life who's getting ready to have her breastbone sawed open? I guess I'd talk about my great dress find, too. After trying hard to be friendly, I finally gave up. "Cathy, please leave. I'm not able to deal with guests tonight." I felt bad but was so consumed with what was looming ahead that I couldn't tolerate any shallow chit-chat, especially about senseless clothes shopping. When you're in a crisis facing life-threatening things, what you want to hear is hope. Whether you have faith or not, you want to hear about God and hope, even if you have never had any thought about them before then. I don't remember anyone talking about that to me—about God—or praying for me. I hope there were people who did. I'm sure there were, but I just didn't realize it. I wonder what difference that would have made for me.

Surgery was scheduled for very early the next morning. Judy, my morning nurse, came in and gave me a wonderful sedative that took the edge off what was coming next. I could have kissed her. My nerves now were hanging on the outside of my skin. All night, tick tock, tick tock, I was ready for any drugs in their arsenal. As the sedative began to work, I felt euphoric, like walking on air with the sun in my face. That is why drugs are bad; you feel too good. Every last problem in the world disappears—even going into surgery to have your chest opened up. *Give me more, please.*

They wheeled me into a very cold, large, green room with enough technology and people for a lively party. I'm so glad I was not in my right mind at that point because it would have been very frightening, all those attendants in green gowns, faces covered, just the eyes poking out. So many metal machines and tubes and wires and tape. Yikes! When I woke up, a man in a white lab coat was seated at the end of my bed, my parents behind him and John beside me. I was so out of it, not sure who he was, and really didn't care. I was having the sweetest sleep of my life. *Don't bother me, anyone.* The doctor kept moving my leg to wake me up, announcing, "You have Hodgkin's disease."

Thankfully, I didn't really care yet because the drugs had not worn off. When I came to completely, he said again, "You have Hodgkin's disease." Hodgkin's disease—the magazine article from the pool friend. "I have good news and bad news for you. The good news is that if you do chemotherapy, you have an 80 percent chance of living. The bad news is that without chemotherapy, you will die."

I was so overwhelmed and foggy that I could not even think clearly enough to ask questions. I just nodded my head okay. After asking him when I would begin the chemotherapy, he answered, "Immediately."

As it turns out, the surgeon did not open my breastbone to peel off the tumor as planned. Instead, because of the symptoms I had described to him the previous week at his office, he had opted to first do a biopsy through my ribs and wait for the results before proceeding. He later told me this decision probably saved my life. Since my breastbone hadn't been opened, I could start chemotherapy immediately rather than having to wait to heal from the planned surgery.

God was orchestrating all my circumstances, from a friend at the pool who read about my symptoms, to meeting the heart surgeon and sharing those symptoms. God was saving my life, unbeknownst to me.

I was suddenly so afraid of everything. I didn't know how I would feel after having poison pumped into my veins, and I was told that the chemotherapy was a very strong regimen that would take me to the brink of death. Since cancer cells grow faster than other cells, the chemotherapy was designed to kill all the faster growing cells in my body without killing me, we hoped. It had been just three days since my surgery when, the next morning, a very businesslike nurse walked into my hospital room. I'm going to call her Mrs. Personality because she was so cheerful and happy—not! She hung a bag of yellow fluid and attached it to my IV. It was this or death, as I had been told by my oncologist. Yes, I now had a cancer doctor, so I sucked it up. As the fluid made its way into my veins, I could taste it. It tasted like Windex smells.

My head began to buzz—another very weird sensation. I felt as if I were standing on one of those vibrating machines. Then, as promised, I started vomiting. It was constant for about eight hours, and then it slowed a bit. I'm so grateful I was in the hospital. A new nurse came in, and a young, compassionate woman gave me some anti-nausea medicine that did little for my symptoms. All this would become my new normal.

When I left the hospital five days later, I was at such a loss. I was afraid of dying, and my body felt so ill. The experience over the last few days had caused me to think deeply about life, death, religion, God, and heaven. What was it all about? I had been through hell and back in the last few weeks. Nana would have said it was all going to be okay, that God was taking care of me. But I didn't know Nana's God.

John and I had visited a large nondenominational church right before my cancer journey began, but we were not churchgoers at all. This crisis put church and God on the forefront of my mind, and maybe for the first time ever, I was thinking seriously about God and heaven. Being faced with death really shook my world and turned it on its head, making me look seriously at eternal life.

I had been raised Catholic, Nana and I taking the city bus to church every Sunday, and John had been raised in the United Church of Christ. Neither of us cared much about church or had any interest in personal faith, but when John's friend and coworker invited us to church, we had felt obligated to go. The message that day was about giving your money to the church—for instance, if you have an RV, you should give it to the church. That's all we both heard, anyway. I'm sure it wasn't said that way, but that's what our ears heard. We both agreed we would not be going back there.

After my diagnosis, I found myself needing answers about God and heaven. What was it all about? What was the truth?

"John, can you get me an appointment with the pastor at that church we visited a few months ago? You know, the one Jim wanted us to visit. I want to know how to get to heaven." I wanted to know what the truth was like Nana knew. Since I hadn't visited any Catholic churches since we moved to Indianapolis, only that nondenominational church, by default that pastor was the only one I knew about in the area. Besides, I really didn't care what anyone thought about my inquiry. I just needed to know what the truth was. Having been raised Catholic, I had been taught that if I was a good person and baptized as an infant, I would go to heaven. Check. Check. The question that kept coming to me was what exactly was good enough? Did I make the standard? I certainly was not Mother Teresa, so how good did I have to be? I just didn't know. The rubber had hit the road for me, and I needed to know what the truth was.

John got the appointment, and the pastor invited us to sit down in his office. I was so grateful to my wonderful husband for helping me navigate through all this uncharted territory. It was an intimidating room, not because of the pastor but because he was a religious authority. In the Catholic church, I had only seen the priest at the altar, removed from the people with his special robes on and a very scholarly look. The pastor had many shelves of books, a large formal cherry desk, and warm lighting. It was a very cozy room, not small but warm—someplace you'd want to put your hat down and stay awhile. In the Catholic church, we were never allowed near the altar where the priest stood. Yet here I was sitting in front of this pastor, asking him how to get to heaven. The whole thing was an out-of-body experience.

"What can I do for you, Cindy?" the pastor asked.

"Well, Pastor Dennis," (in Catholic church, it was *Father* Dennis) "I was hoping you could answer an important question about how to get to heaven."

He picked up his black leather Bible, pliable like Play-Doh and worn to the point of cracking. By the condition of it, he must have paged through that book millions of times. He opened it to the book of John. I remember Nana reading her Bible and saying the rosary, talking to God, but no one had ever opened a Bible for me. Only the priests had read from the Bible at my church, and Nana had her own worn-out Bible.

He pointed at John 3:16 and asked me to read it. Wow! I had never read anything in the Bible before. This was really legit. It said, "For God so loved the world that he gave his one and only Son, that whoever believes in him shall not perish but have eternal life." Access to eternal life was exactly what I wanted to find, but I still had questions. "What does that mean?"

"It means that God loves you so much, Cindy," Pastor Dennis said, "that he was willing to have his one and only Son die for you, and that by believing in God's Son, Jesus, you can have eternal life."

I guess I believed that Jesus is God's Son, but somehow I thought there'd be more to believing than simply saying that I believe Jesus is God's Son and that he died for me. I also didn't know what to do with my thoughts about having to be a good person and going to church and confession. I was on a mission, and I really didn't care about what the pastor thought of me. I wasn't embarrassed as I would have been if I wasn't so desperate, if I didn't feel my life was on the line. My need to know far exceeded how I felt right then or what I thought anyone might be thinking about me.

He took me to another passage, Ephesians 2:8–9. "For it is by grace you have been saved, through faith—and this is not from yourselves, it is a gift of God—not by works, so that no one can boast." Pastor Dennis explained that it's not by being a good person but by believing in God's Son, Jesus, and putting him in charge of my life that I would gain eternal life in heaven. It was the whole "putting him in charge of my life" part that I had been missing.

It was a great relief that going to heaven wasn't about being a good person because I had not been as good as Mother Teresa, and I had no idea how I could become good enough or even what good enough was. My questions were being answered. It wasn't about goodness and who's good enough; it was all about what Jesus had already done. But it just seemed too easy. Mother Teresa worked so hard all her life, not for herself but for others. This was certainly not true for me.

The pastor explained that the problem is holiness. Only God is holy, and we are all sinners. (Did you ever think badly about someone? Well, that's sin.) We can't be in heaven with God without being holy. How do we become holy? God made the way by having Jesus pay our sins' price for us. That's what Easter is all about. That death is what provided us the path to eternal life in heaven. I was learning something so important; it's not about goodness but about believing. So by giving Jesus access to the driver's seat of my life, I began to *want* to do good things, not to earn my way to heaven. Jesus had already taken care of that. Many of my questions had now been answered, but I needed time to think everything through. It was all so much and so new.

It reminds me now of the story about twins talking in their mother's womb. One twin asks, "Did you know that when we're born, there's a whole world out there for us to experience? Bright sunshine, oceans, mountains, people, and birds of every color—even whales."

"Hogwash," the other twin says. "You're crazy. This is all there is, our dark, watery womb."

I was beginning to experience a world outside a watery womb, and it was thrilling. John and I began reading the Bible together, beginning with the book of John. Then Pastor Dennis came to visit us. I later found out that his son had Hodgkin's disease and was going through chemotherapy in Arkansas while I was having treatment in Indianapolis. What are the chances of that? I can only imagine how much he longed to care for his son as he was going through this terrible disease. Although he couldn't be with his son whom he dearly missed and was suffering with, he could be with us. That fact was amazing to me. God was going before Pastor Dennis and me, putting it all together perfectly. First Thessalonians 5:18 tells us to give thanks because giving thanks is God's will for us in Christ Jesus. Romans 8:28 tells us that we know that he works everything out for the good of those who love him.

CHAPTER TWO

Treatment

For 10 very long months, I fought like a boxer in the ring, one blow after another, bloody and swollen but still getting up. The chemo was strong, poisonous, and strenuous, leaving me so weak that John had to physically carry me to weekly doctors' appointments. I weighed less than I did when I was 12 years old. On the way to my treatments, I would start vomiting in the car. John's car had that new car smell—like Windex, the thing I tasted when the chemo rushed through my veins. I guess just the thought of it would get me hurling. My doctor said this would happen: "It's subliminal, like Pavlov's dogs from science class."

That will never happen to me, I'd foolishly thought at the time. *I have an iron stomach, and it just won't happen.* Yet there we were in the exam room, and I was vomiting even though I hadn't received the treatment yet. "John, get the garbage can. I have to vomit." It was all just as Dr. Bruce said it would be.

My regimen for treatment was the standard for Hodgkin's disease: an IV chemotherapy every two weeks and chemotherapy pills on the off days. It was a grueling schedule. For eight months, my bed was my home. I cared little about anything else. It was hard to get up, and I was nauseous all the time. I vomited every day for a full year. I felt weak, thin, depressed, hopeless, and completely lifeless. Days had become so burdensome for John and me. He cared for me while working on his new career, and I lay in bed sick. It wasn't the way a newly married couple should be living, not like that enchanting summer dinner we'd shared with our friends just months earlier.

My bed was unsatisfying. When you crawl into bed at the end of a great day, it's oh so gratifying. But such gratification was a distant memory. The bed made me achy and uncomfortable. I longed for that feeling of crawling into bed and sighing because it felt so good to lie down after a long, active day.

We had two small cocker spaniels, Panda and Peaches. They were so sweet. Neither left my bedside. We loved them, but since I couldn't care for them, they became another burden for John. With three flights of stairs to potty them, many days were arduous. The good outweighed the bad, though, because Panda and Peaches became real companions to John when I couldn't be present. He thoroughly enjoyed their distinct personalities. Panda would cuddle on his lap, and Peaches would demand his attention, poking at him whenever he sat down, as if to say, "Please pet me! Give me love!" God knew we needed those pups to encourage our despairing hearts. Nothing like a puppy's face to cheer you on.

After six long months, our enthusiasm rose as we anticipated only two more months of treatments. Finally, after many long, difficult, grueling months, we could see the finish line. At my scheduled doctor's appointment, I mentally skipped into the treatment room, knowing the end was near. Then Dr. Bruce stopped my skipping in its tracks. "Cindy, I've met with the board over your treatment plan, and based on your most recent CAT scan, it looks like we will have to do another eight months of chemotherapy." *No! No! No!* There was no way I could handle any more chemotherapy. I weighed nothing and was so weak. I could barely leave my bed now. I knew in my heart I would die if I put any more chemo into my body. I just did not have it in me; I had no will to live through more chemo. The wicked mustard gas chemicals had done a real trick on my frail body. My arms couldn't even open because the harsh but life-saving chemicals had hardened my veins. Imagine poisonous drugs designed to kill cells yet save lives. Sounds like an oxymoron. *No! No! No!*

I've heard it said that God doesn't give us more than we can handle, but that was hard to believe at that point. I think it's more accurate to say that God may give you more than you can handle if it's necessary, but he will always get you through. Nana believed that wholeheartedly.

I struggled that week with the news because I was convinced I could not last another eight months. I understood why people sometimes say no to more treatment. You just know your limit, even when your life is at stake.

Although I didn't really understand what I was reading, I began reading the Bible, trying to understand what God was like. I wanted to know if God was really there caring for me or if he was in heaven, just beginning and ending lives. I prayed silently that I would not have to go through what the doctors had already said was necessary.

Then a miracle happened, as Nana would say. At my next appointment, Dr. Bruce said that after discussing my case again with his oncology group, they concluded that I should stick with the original protocol—no extension. In my head, I was skipping, dancing, jumping all around the room. How thrilling God was to show me that he really was involved in my care. I began to recognize his involvement in my healing. He was answering my lame, pitiful attempts at personal prayer that was different from the "Our Fathers" I had known before. I learned that prayer was like talking to my friend who loves me.

"Honey, the doorbell is ringing. Can you get it?" I called to John from the bedroom.

"Hello, Pastor Dennis," I heard John say.

Great, I thought. My apartment was a mess. Peaches had torn my newspaper, and I'd let her have fun. Pastor Dennis was a man of the cloth—that's what we called the priests, anyway. I still had that reverent authority for a pastor. Quickly, I dressed and came out to help John host him. The pastor was special to me because of all the questions he'd answered on my journey for truth on how to get to heaven.

"Pastor Dennis, how are you?" I shook his hand. "Thank you for stopping by to check on me."

He returned the greeting and then got right to business. "Cindy, John, I have something I want to talk with you about."

What could he possibly want to speak to us about?

"John, Cindy, the Bible talks about getting baptized. We have a pool in our church where we do baptisms on Sunday."

A pool? I was sprinkled at Sacred Heart of Jesus, so I was good to go, right? But then he asked if we could be baptized on Sunday.

"No, thank you, Pastor Dennis. I've already been baptized at Sacred Heart and John at his little church in Wisconsin."

But he insisted that I needed to be fully submerged in their baptismal during a Sunday morning service, regardless of my infant baptism. At this particular church, they believed that to truly become a Christian, you had to be baptized by full immersion. If you professed faith in Jesus but were never fully submerged in baptism, you would be rejected by God and spend eternity in hell. That's strong language, but it's what this particular church believed.

Although his words were frightening, I had bigger problems. I had a Hickman catheter, the kind used to deliver chemotherapy, hanging out of my chest. Dr. Bruce had told me not to get the Hickman wet. I had to tape it up every time I showered. "We don't want a bacterial infection happening with your extremely low immune system," he'd said. "That could be deadly for you." So there was simply no way I was getting into that pool. The pastor and I were facing a huge dilemma. I was afraid of infection and possible death, and he was afraid of my dying and going to hell because I wasn't baptized. Looking back, his fear trumped mine. This battle went on for months, fueled by his burden for me to be baptized and my desire to avoid the water.

Today, having spent years reading God's Word for myself, I now know that baptism doesn't get you to heaven—only belief in Jesus does that (Rom. 10:9). Baptism is a demonstrated act of obedience that God calls us to after we receive him as Savior, after having put him in the driver's seat of our life, after confessing with our mouth that Jesus is Lord and believing in our heart that God raised him from the dead. In Matthew 28:19–20, Jesus talks about baptism when making disciples.

After the doctors removed my catheter, it was safe for me to be baptized. I found myself wanting to do this thing that God had asked me to do—to be baptized by full immersion. Because I'd asked Jesus to have complete control over my life and had committed to putting him in the driver's seat, my baptism that particular Sunday marks the day of my salvation. I remember it like it was yesterday. I became the passenger in the car. Jesus was now the driver of my new life. After I was baptized, my prior sins flooded my mind, and I confessed them, never to look back on them again, just as God won't. Jesus cast my past sins "as far as the east is from the west" (Ps. 103:12). God says my sins are completely forgotten and removed.

It was a wonderful, inspiring day, yet it was sad. It was wonderful because I was beginning my new life with Jesus but sad because I knew I had to change some unhealthy aspects of my life, even at the cost of losing some friends. My friends were familiar and fun, and Jesus was new and unknown. With God driving the car, I was embarking on a new journey into new territory.

Thirty years have passed since that day, but now John and I can see how God is truly a master at making himself known to us. Learning to rely on God was a new adventure for us, but he brought wonderful teachers and counselors, from television preachers and radio broadcasters to Christian YouTube videos. I'm coming to understand God's words, and I find them fascinating. I'm beginning to realize that I can't live this life without him. The Lord has been so incredibly wonderful to me. I'm seeing how he wants to give me inexhaustible treasures every day—beautiful, valuable riches of treasure. "The kingdom of heaven is like treasure hidden in a field. When a man found it, he hid it again, and then in his joy went and sold all he had and bought that field" (Matt. 13:44). I want to seek him and find him through all the avenues he offers me—through Bible studies, preachers, Christian music, and friends who know him better than I do to find those good treasures in every single circumstance.

We are never alone. The one who holds the stars in the sky is carrying us right now. As we dig into his Word and let the pages come alive, Jesus brings us closer to him. God has been holding me in his hands and helping me. He said in Isaiah 41:13, "For I am the LORD your God who takes hold of your right hand and says to you, Do not fear; I will help you." Even before I knew him, I could see the evidence of his working on my behalf—how I sought him and he answered me, how he delivered me from all my fears, and how he saved me from all my troubles (Ps. 34).

I see God carrying me and directing every circumstance for my good—from early me bringing a friend with me to the doctor, to the doctor not opening my breastbone because I tipped him off about a friend's magazine article that highlighted Hodgkin's disease symptoms. First Thessalonians 5:18 says to "give thanks in all circumstances, for this is God's will for you." Romans 8:28 says he works everything out "for the good of those who love him." Although we can make our own plans, he establishes our steps (Prov. 16:9). He's here, always working and caring for my best interest according to his plans for me, even against my own plans, even in the dreadful times.

John Piper, a pastor and writer (and my mentor, though he doesn't even know who I am), gave this illustration in a March 12, 2018, interview called "Gods Sovereign Plans behind Your Most Unproductive Days."

Your priority may be that between 10:00 and 11:00 this morning you plan to run to the bank and get some cash so that you can be back in time to pay the teenager who is cutting your grass while a neighbor watches your two- and four-year-old for you. That's the plan....

However, God has a totally different set of priorities.

Your neighbor was scheduled to be at a real estate office at 11:30 so she could join her husband to close on a new house—a house that, unbeknownst to them, has a flawed foundation. The teenager was planning to take his money from cutting the grass and pool it with some of the guys and buy some drugs that they shouldn't be using. You hit a traffic jam caused by the rollover of a semi (which has another story behind it). You're locked up on the freeway for an hour. You never even get to the bank.

You rush home as fast as you can, but you get there an hour late. You have no money to pay the boy, and your neighbor has missed her appointment. You are frustrated almost to tears.

Your efficiency proved utterly useless to accomplish your priorities. You failed, but God's priorities totally succeeded. He wanted to hinder that boy from buying drugs, he wanted to spare the neighbor from purchasing a house that's a lemon, and he wanted to grow your faith in his sovereign wisdom and sovereignty.

Now, that's what I mean by "God's priorities for efficiency in this life are not ours."[1]

---

1. John Piper, "God's Sovereign Plans behind Your Most Unproductive Days," Desiring God, https://www.desiringgod.org/interviews/gods-sovereign-plans-behind-your-most-unproductive-days.

Looking back on my cancer and surgery from God's perspective, I'd say that the doctor's priority for me was to undergo the surgery, cut open my breastbone, and peel off the tumor. But God's priority was to protect me from that surgery—maybe because if I had died during that operation, I would not have gone to heaven to live with him. I did not have that life-saving faith yet. I had not put him in the driver's seat, but despite all that, God was in the center all along, protecting me and wanting to bring me comfort.

The book of Job tells us that God delivers people in their suffering and "speaks to them in their affliction. He is wooing you from the jaws of distress to a spacious place free from restriction, to the comfort of your table laden with choice food" (Job 36:15–16). Don't you love that word *wooing*? I want to be wooed by God. Don't you? I want to be wooed to a spacious place with no restrictions. I want freedom from worry and being terrified. I want to eat at Jesus's table of choice food prepared for me by God himself. Nothing could be more beneficial or more important to me.

Before my diagnosis, I was living life for today and for myself, thinking such living was the ultimate dream. I didn't know about God holding me, carrying me, delivering me, wooing me, and bringing me wonderful, choice food. I can picture it now—a huge, beautifully decorated table with white linen tablecloths. Jesus likes white, and he's very fond of linen in the Bible. There are baskets (something else he likes) of warm, crusty, homemade bread, the aroma filling the entire banquet hall, served with the most expensive olive oil. Large goblets of dark red wine fermented and breathed from the finest winery. Filet mignon with a cognac truffle mushroom sauce and pearl shallots smothering the steak. Am I making my point here? You fill in your table and dream. Child of God, dream, for the Father has been pleased to give you the kingdom.

I didn't know all this then. I never looked at God's Word or knew that all those verses were there for me. I didn't know that he wrote his book for me to read and understand so I could know this incredible love and care that God has for me. He watches over me, helps me, and solves all my problems—even problems I had no idea existed. I didn't know Jesus wanted to be my personal Savior. I didn't even see how faith could help me, but the astonishing thing was that Jesus was looking over me all that time anyway. He had the entire plan for this already worked out in my life, even when I completely ignored him.

It reminds me of when I was in India and saw a young man—a shepherd, a herder of sheep—walking down a dirt road with all his sheep in tow. He had a large staff he used to keep them tightly herded together. It was quite a fascinating thing to watch. How those sheep stayed in line with his lead was very remarkable. Around his neck, an infant lamb was draped just like a towel after a run. I figured the young lamb must have been too tired to walk. Watching this made me think of what God does for you and me. Sometimes we carry a boatload of burdens on our shoulders—the weight of the world. Ever been there? We work as hard as we can to figure it all out, to solve the seemingly impossible problems, only to throw our hands in the air hopelessly because we have no solution, no answer, no revelation for our struggle, only a painful uncertainty of just how lost we are— similar to the young lamb.

We ask God, "Where are you? What am I supposed to do?" He seems silent. No answer comes, just an empty void. It's at that moment the Great Shepherd of our souls grabs our weary bodies and flings us around his neck. The Lord says, "I am the good Shepherd, and if you will let me, I'm going to lift you on my strong, capable shoulders and carry these burdens for you. Child, I never intended for you to carry them. I who never sleeps or slumbers will take care of you." And then he says, "My yolk is easy and my burden is light" (Matt. 11:30). That two-ton weight on our backs should begin to slip right off as we let go of the reins and put God in the driver's seat of our problems.

I lift up my eyes to the mountains—
    where does my help come from?
My help comes from the LORD,
    the Maker of heaven and earth.

—Ps. 121:1–2

Have you ever sat and looked at a huge mountain? It's incredible, majestic, and powerful. There was once a tribal people who lived next to a huge mountain. The town greatly feared that mountain. I can see why. It's an intimidating, awesome sight. God made that mountain. He who made it "will not let your foot slip—he who watches over you will not slumber; indeed, he who watches over Israel will neither slumber nor sleep" (Ps. 121:3–4).

The LORD will keep you from all harm—
    he will watch over your life;
the LORD will watch over your coming and going
    both now and forevermore.

—Ps. 121:7–8

I'm beginning to understand God more fully; he really is carrying me during those most difficult times. I love the stories in the Bible because they show me who God is, who he made me to be, and how he cares for and loves each of us.

The more aware I am of God's presence in my circumstances, the safer I feel. Feeling God's presence with me is not some sort of escape from reality; rather, it's a turning toward the ultimate reality. Jesus is becoming far more real to me than the world I see, hear, and touch. Thirty years of getting to know him have surely proved that.

CHAPTER THREE

It's Not Fair

A few years later, Hodgkin's disease was no longer my elephant in the room. I wasn't dominated by the thought of cancer and chemo, and my health was stable. I was feeling what we all call normal. My passions were resurfacing, and excitement filled my heart. There was a future ahead, and my new driver, Jesus, was leading the way. Sure, I'd had cancer, past tense, but I could think about dresses and shopping again. Since I had put some weight back on, the dressing room wasn't a thing I avoided at all costs anymore. John and I found ourselves in what we call our happy place—a euphoric, light, freewheeling state of mind.

"Honey, where do you see us in five years?" John asked one night. "Imagine this, Cindy. We're playing soccer on the front lawn of our newly purchased, sprawling, ranch-style home with our son and daughter giggling at how weird we are."

"Wow! That's a superb thought, honey," I said with a laugh. "It has been four years now, and I do see all our friends pregnant or with toddlers in tow. Have you noticed that?"

"Yes. I watch Kevin with his boys, and I want that."

I took his hand. "Aw, honey. Me too."

We had been so absorbed in my fight for life in hospitals and chemotherapy that we'd forgotten about the world going on around us. Our plates had been spilling over with health crises, and we had forgotten the existence of a delightfully pleasant community right in front of us. "This feels so good, doesn't it?" I said. "No more blood count charts or anti-nausea medicines sitting on our kitchen table. We can actually consider dinner plans with friends and engaging in the world going on around us." We could talk about how good the cream of mushroom soup was or whether we should see the latest action movie at the theater. We could reminisce about the gold Trans Am purchase we'd made because we didn't know any better.

At our favorite Mexican spot with cha-cha music blaring and bowls bursting with warm corn chips, John finally asked outright, "Honey, what do you think about us having a baby?"

"You seem excited, and I'm getting excited."

"Let's do it!"

"Really? You think you're ready for that?" I could tell he was apprehensive, yet I could hear excitement in his voice. His clock was ticking, too.

"Honey," he said, "that is what I call living a perfectly normal life, us planning a marvelous future. You know, Dr. Bruce is okay with us having children. If he's okay, let us be okay." We celebrated the evening, lingering until the last chip was gone and our stomachs were exploding. It was a great night.

I'd always dreamed of having a baby, so after that memorable Mexican dinner conversation, I prayed to become pregnant. "God, please, could I get pregnant? I would love to have a big, fat belly for people to rub, and I want to wear those hip, trendy baby bump clothes. I want to feel my child when he moves inside of me. I hope you give me a boy, Lord. I want the whole pregnancy experience."

Everything baby was exciting to me. I was obsessed with every little gadget and must-have trend for infants. Searching the web and blogs, I tried to learn everything there was to know about the newest, latest, greatest baby paraphernalia. John was having his own excitement over our idea of a child. We felt it was a brilliant plan to start a family.

Quickly, we realized it wasn't going to be as easy for us as it seemed for every other normal, childbearing person on the planet. We did everything we could, down to recording my ovulation cycle on chart after chart to determine when I was most fertile. Our efforts yielded only frustration. The lack of spontaneity and recording every intimate moment got old fast.

"What could be the problem, honey?" John asked. "Maybe we should consult with a professional." He was smart to not use the word *doctor*, but still, I winced.

Yuck! No more doctors. No way! The last thing I wanted was to see another exam room and white-coat medical team. At the same time, I did really, really want to be pregnant. So the question became if I was willing to go through appointments, exam rooms, doctors, nurses, shots, and medicine. Was I willing to feel horrible again to increase my chances of becoming pregnant? The desire for a baby was growing inside me—one I could feel kicking and rolling around. It was becoming more compelling with each passing moment. With time, my baby dreams began to outweigh my distain over the dark visions of exam rooms and white coats. I imagined how women might question me at the mall. "When are you due? What are you naming your child? Have you thought about colors and the theme of your baby's room?" I was getting chills just thinking about it. How thrilling! I was loving my mommy daydreaming. I would think about talking with all my friends and sharing the details of my pregnancy with them. I was ready. "John, I think exam rooms and white coats are worth it. Let's do it. I'll call the doctor in the morning to get an appointment."

We met with my first white-coat gynecologist who put me on a fertility drug. I felt hopeful. Surely this would work for us. Leaving the office, we were giddy and making cute remarks about having a baby.

"I wonder what we'll have," John said.

"Surely a curious, adventurous boy just like you, although I hope he has the fix-it gene."

"Well, I'm hoping for a ruffled ballerina who loves tchotchkes on her wrists and has bows in her hair just like you."

A day turned into a week, and a week became a month. There were still no signs of pregnancy, and it felt like every person on God's green earth was pregnant except me. My best friend was pregnant again with child number *two*. I could feel myself spiraling down into a pit of despair. My world darkened as I retreated into my cocoon. I had been there before when Dr. Bruce said I had to go through another eight months of chemo. I began avoiding happy social activities like having lunch downtown or going to Susie's spin class. My poor John tried everything to stop this miserable pity party I was participating in, but I couldn't be consoled. I had big dreams to fulfill and baby gadgets to buy. What an enormous emotional drop, back to ground zero, negative zero, nothing. Why did I let myself dream so huge? This was a colossal letdown. I'd put all my eggs in one basket, my daydreaming basket.

I couldn't believe I wasn't getting pregnant. What a debacle my life had become. I'd believed—wholeheartedly believed beyond a shadow of doubt, no question about it—that my good God was going to give me a baby. Everybody gets a baby—even those who don't want one. God wouldn't do this to me after all I'd been through. I guess I thought I'd had my bad, so now I should get my heart's desires.

John was tremendously supportive and not nearly as impatient as I had become, saying things like, "Honey, everything will work out." His leadership style is to always be hopeful and confident, even when he's not feeling it. I really needed his support. To me, that's the best leader of all—confident under pressure and emotional turmoil. The process had to affect him, too, but it hardly showed. While his wife was a basket case, falling apart at the seams, all he wanted to do was make her happy.

Dear reader, if you have been through this process, you know how emotionally devastating each fertility cycle can be—chart after chart, week after week of wanting and waiting for something that just is not happening. And then there's the complete letdown each time you realize you're not pregnant. It's exhausting and emotionally depressing for both husband and wife.

Finally, we exhausted the fertility-pill route. It was time to decide if we wanted to take the next step, going to a fertility clinic for more extensive procedures.

"Do I even have it in me to do this?" I asked aloud.

"Cindy, we've already invested every emotion into having a baby," John said. "So at what point do we say no more?"

"I don't know."

"Let's just talk with the clinic and see what they propose. We've come this far."

John can be so steady and logical at times. How could I say no? The process was grueling and very mechanical, but this clinic had such a high success rate that we felt we should at least try it.

Again, we experienced charts and drugs and wanting and waiting and disappointment after disappointment. The infertility specialist finally recommended surgery for answers, and I went in the following Thursday morning for exploratory surgery. I couldn't believe I was going in for an elective operation, but I needed answers. I felt sucked into a deep black hole, the must-have-a-baby abyss again, and there was no way out unless I made a move forward. *Where are you, God?*

"Cindy," Dr. Jarrett said, "I'm sorry to tell you that you are in menopause, and all your eggs are gone. You will not be able to have children."

What? That was impossible. Here I was again with I'm-way-too-young-for-these ailments. I was only 29.

"Are you saying I cannot get pregnant, ever?" I felt like I was going to spill my insides right there on the shiny tile floor. Blood drained from my face. I'd been here before. I bent my head down between my legs and sobbed uncontrollably. My dreams snapped like twigs in a hurricane—and I've seen hurricane devastation. *How could this be? Why, God? Why? No child of my own to hold and nurture in my arms? It makes no sense. Where are you, God?*

I could feel my face turning red-hot with anger, and I profusely refused to accept this heart-wrenching news. I wanted to stomp my feet like a toddler not getting her way and have a complete tantrum. How could God do this to me? I know you're involved in this, God. You have to get in my mind. Remind me, Lord. Please, please give me clarity. You say you give me what's best for me, and you say you love me (Lam. 3:25). I don't understand why you would prevent me from having children. What's the point? Do you want me to give up on you, give up on believing that you're caring for me and that no one could take better care of me than you? (Ps. 34:5). You know the beginning and the end of life. All my days are ultimately in your hands. Every split second is controlled by you, but this feels out of bounds. This feels like punishment, Lord. I cannot see a single positive, hopeful thing here, no good thing at all. To take away my very life's dream—why? It doesn't make sense. I shouldn't be mad at you. You're my Creator, my heavenly Father, the one who sustains me. You're the one who holds all things together with your voice. You love me with an everlasting love that no one else possesses or can even come close to. It sounds so ridiculous to say all I know about your goodness to me, but I'm just so worn-down from having to trust you with all these devastating things that you keep bringing into my life. I just can't see any good things coming my way.

I later found out that it's normal to become infertile after chemotherapy, especially the kind of chemotherapy I had been given. Today, oncologists will often harvest some of your eggs before they start treatment.

I was absolutely heartbroken—weak, tired, hopeless, and numb that I would never be able to have a child. I had put *all* my hope in these fertility doctors and procedures as the way God was working for me. It had been an emotional roller-coaster ride, and the money—we had spent so much money—had resulted in nothing. The clinic had such a high success rate and had helped so many women get pregnant. Our doctor even had the leading rate of babies born from infertility, so of course, we had believed it would work for us. Nope, not for me. It was impossible for me. I kept asking why and kept getting no answer. After my battle through cancer, I knew in my heart that God would make this okay somehow, yet my desperation kept me from believing that he could still have a plan for John and me to have a baby. Simply put, I wanted my way. It was the only option I could see for myself.

I can honestly say I would have done anything to have a child. Settling was not in my vocabulary, so when our fertility doctor initially gave us some hope, we snatched it. Since we now knew that I had no eggs, Dr. Jarrett offered us the option of using another woman's eggs (donor eggs). I could still become pregnant, just not with my own egg or genes. The growing baby would be a combination of John's genes and some other woman's genes, conceived in a petri dish. It sounded far-fetched, a little sci-fi to me, and I wasn't crazy about the idea, but in my desperation, everything seemed doable to me. Others had done it, so why not me? John and I had been through so much together, and since he wanted children, too, he was willing to give me this. He also saw it as doable. When you feel desperate, you do desperate things.

We began the process. After the doctor found a surrogate who looked like me, the next step was to take John's sperm and the donor's eggs and let them conceive in a petri dish. When the call came, we were told that the conception had been unsuccessful.

Surprisingly, we both felt this was good news. Secretly, we both felt uneasy after the procedure. I felt John would have a connection to this other woman who had donated her eggs. I was growing extremely uncomfortable with the situation and more than a little jealous. John thought it was too out there and not natural as he thought God intended.

If the eggs had been fertilized, our fertility doctors had planned to have the unused eggs frozen somewhere in a storage container. The clinics dictate all kinds of rules, protocols, ethics, and issues with leftover fertilized eggs. We believe that our uneasy feelings were reflections of God's providence because we later learned that those frozen embryos would have been in violation of what God says in his Word about when conception begins. In hindsight, we saw God working to protect us from emotional heartache and guilt over not following his plans for our life. Seems to me that God had the best plan all along, a plan I didn't even know I would benefit from later in my life. I've learned from the Bible that life really does begin at conception, so I could never abort by disposing a petri dish baby. That baby would still be a baby in God's eyes and now in my eyes, too. I'm so grateful to God for helping me through this process. He delivered me from my own self. God was kind and gracious even in my ignorance.

Let me pause to say that if you have a child through this process, thank God for his provision, because his plans extend far beyond our limited understanding of his ways. His works are perfect, and all his ways are just. He is a faithful God who does no wrong. If you have aborted a baby, God's forgiveness, grace, and unimaginable love are available to you. Let the Father pour over any hurt you may have in this area of your life. Talk to him about it. He's the great physician of all your wounds—physical, mental, and spiritual. Talk with him just as you talk with your friend. Tell him how you feel, and let him put some healing ointment into any wounds you may have over this sorrow.

I have met so many women who suffer from having had an abortion. I'm here to say that you don't have to because that aborted child is in the heavenly Father's hands today. I'm so glad they get to live in a tranquil paradise with Jesus and never spend one moment in this less-than-perfect world. Ask the Lord to forgive you, and he will cast that sin so far away that he won't even see it anymore (Ps. 103:12). He doesn't relive it; so, dear friend, you don't need to relive it, either.

As for me, I thank God for not letting the petri dish baby take place. At the time, I thought it would be a great thing, but God, who knows all, knew it would hurt John and me in the end.

Again, I was desperate. I had given myself over to a baby at any cost. I thought every day, all day long, about how I could get pregnant. I had lost my God compass that pointed me to his plan for my best; instead, I lived with an I-must-have-it mentality. What was I thinking? All on my own, I had made myself miserable.

Reading in the Bible, I was struck by the similarities between me and a woman named Sarah, the wife of Abraham. She was a lovely woman of God who, like me, desperately wanted children, even though it seemed like she and Abraham would never conceive. In the midst of their infertility, something amazing happened. The Lord spoke to Abraham and promised him that he and Sarah would have a son despite their infertility.

Wonderful! And they all lived happily ever after, right? After all, God had promised the birth of a child. But no. Years passed, and by the time Sarah was 90, she still had not had a child. Imagine how desperate she must have felt and what an outcast she must have been. All her friends were likely grandparents by now, and the Bible says her womb and Abraham's body were as good as dead. Wow! Talk about an impossible situation. Eventually, Sarah reached a breaking point and concluded that God was not going to come through on his promise.

Having decided that she couldn't trust God's plan to be in her best interest, Sarah devised her own plan. She told her husband, "The Lord has kept me from having children. Go, sleep with my slave; perhaps I can build a family through her" (Gen. 16:2). Sadly, back then women did this kind of thing with their slaves. Can you sense her despair? How miserable she must have been to suggest such a thing. Here's the kicker, though. Abraham agreed to the plan. Maybe Sarah wore him down, and he just gave in. Or maybe he was like John and so desperately wanted this for his wife. Either way, it seemed a reasonable plan to Abraham and similar to how Adam went along with Eve's idea to eat from the forbidden tree in the garden. Only God knows our *why*.

Sarah's plan turned out to be a terrible idea. She took her Egyptian slave Hagar and gave her to Abraham. He slept with Hagar, and she conceived. When Hagar knew she was pregnant, she began to despise Sarah. When Sarah began blaming Abraham for Hagar's hurtful attitude, he simply put the blame back on Sarah. By deciding she knew best and taking matters into her own hands, Sarah caused herself and others a lot of heartache. Even her husband was done with her, telling her, "Your slave is in your hands" (Gen. 16:6). Yet even after all this drama, God blessed Sarah with a son from her own womb, exactly as he had promised (Gen. 21:1–2). God had been working everything according to his perfect plan all along.

Like Sarah, I could have warded off so much heartache if I had just waited and trusted God. When the donor eggs did not conceive, John and I interpreted the results as God directing us not to pursue this approach to have a child. With the lack of conception and our unsettled feelings about the process, we resolved to put everything back solely in God's hands.

In the months that followed, it was nice to have a break from dwelling on infertility. We felt relief and peace. By giving us a taste of what we thought would make us happy, God had shown us that it was not going to lead to happiness after all, only misery. I wonder if Sarah felt relief when it was all over for her, too.

I have desires—I believe good desires—all day long, and I'm grateful that I can dream. I just need those dreams to be in rhythm with God's plans. The Lord says he gives us the desires of our hearts when those desires are in line with his plans. "Take delight in the Lord, and he will give you the desires of your heart" (Ps. 37:4). As I think about my infertility process, I realize now that there is nothing I could ever know better than what God already knows. *God, please help me to bow my head and say yes, Lord, to whatever changes you want to make in my life, even when I don't understand—or feel like you will come through for me. Lord, adjust my desires to be your desires. Help me to believe the truth, to know you have the most wonderful ultimate plan in mind. Thank you, God, for taking my royal debacle of infertility and turning it on its head, protecting John and me in all of it.*

God's plans are never defeated. He's always accomplishing his purposes for our lives. He is sovereign. Scripture tells us that the Lord does what he pleases with his creation, which includes everything—people, animals, stars, anything you can name. "The LORD does whatever pleases him, in the heavens and on the earth, in the seas and all their depths" (Ps. 135:6). That's how I can have confidence knowing he was involved in my lack of fertilized eggs. There are so many examples of God overtaking our plans for his ultimate plan. We can make our plans, but the Lord determines our steps (Prov. 16:9). Philippians 2:13 says, "For it is God who works in you to will and to act in order to fulfill his good purpose."

Six months after our failed attempt to conceive with a donor egg and still very eager to have a child, John and I sat down to have a conversation about the possible next steps. We went to Sally's, our local café, known for its delectable American pastries. "American" stands for extra-large and loaded with sugary goo. They're made-from-scratch, warm, pull-apart, gooey pastries. That's a really posh way of saying big, fat, scrumptious, melt-in-your-mouth donuts. John especially loves Sally's fresh coffee from Costa Rica. He's an off-the-charts coffee connoisseur—you might say he's a little snobby about it. The café was hustling with locals.

"Cindy, grab that corner spot." John has a way of always securing the best seats anywhere—restaurants, theaters, churches, even airplanes. You name it, he'll find it. I moved quickly through the people and snatched up the cozy corner spot, a perfect place for our serious talk. When he returned from ordering, I congratulated him on the best seats in the house. We snuggled into the comfy leather chairs as our coffee arrived.

"Where do we begin?" I asked.

"I think we are both feeling this need to pursue adoption," John said. "Don't you?" Over the last few months, John and I had sporadically discussed adoption and considered whether God was presenting this idea to us. We had learned that adoption required a lot of work and thought. Finding a baby was like looking for a needle in a haystack. Where would we begin? It was not by coincidence that some friends had introduced us to a prominent adoption attorney in Indianapolis. He told us that we would have to find a child for ourselves. How in the world would we do that? The process, the attorney explained, was to write letters to your friends, letting them know you're looking for a baby. You market yourself so a birth mom will see you and decide you're a good candidate to care for her child forever. That sounded so businesslike and impersonal to us, and beyond that, we doubted if it could actually work.

"But, John," I said. "Talk about a mountain too high to climb. As we have already discussed, it would be like winning the lottery, which would be extra surprising considering we don't play."

"Cindy, I know it seems impossible."

"God is going to have to drop that birth mom into our laps, literally," I said. I needed God to remind me he was the one in control of bringing us our baby if we were going to have one. I'd been through the I-can-do-this-myself route and never wanted to go that route again. It felt like the Sarah and Abraham story all over again. Sarah could not see how it could possibly happen, yet God still gave her a baby even though her womb was as good as dead. The scriptures say that she even laughed at the news of an impending pregnancy. In response to her laughter, God declared, "Is anything too hard for the LORD? I will return to you at the appointed time next year, and Sarah will have a son" (Gen. 18:14).

C. H. Mackintosh sums up my struggle:

> The poor heart naturally prefers anything to the attitude of *waiting*. It will turn to any expedient—any scheme—any resource, rather than be kept in that posture. It is one thing to believe a promise, at the first, and quite another to wait quietly for the accomplishment thereof.[2]

At that warm, wonderful, inviting café, we agreed to pursue adoption. How could we turn down anything after being seduced by those warm pastries? The search went on for only a couple of months before John and I realized we didn't have it in us to actually find a baby. Refusing to get sucked into the I-must-have-a-baby abyss again, we decided to stop the adoption process. That was a hard but relief-filled day. It was hard because the hole was still there. It was filled with relief because the pursuit was emotionally exhausting. We decided it was time again to trust that God would bring us a baby if he wanted us to have one. We realized we needed him to bring us peace and contentment for the baby hole we were in. I found this definition of contentment that I'd love for God to embed deep into my heart: "An inward assurance in God's sovereignty and goodness that produces the fruit of joy, peace, and thanksgiving in the life of a believer regardless of outward circumstances."[3]

We knew that the only action we could take was to trust God to take charge of it for us and refuse the impulse to dwell on the disappointments. In Isaiah 48:17, the Lord tells us, "I am the LORD your God, who teaches you what is best for you, who directs you in the way you should go." Okay, God, you will show us. Every time we

---

2. C. H. Mackintosh, *Notes on the Pentateuch: Genesis to Deuteronomy*, Google Books.
3. Melissa Kruger, "Biblical Contentment," *What Is Biblical Contentment?*, *Session One*. slide presentation, 2018, Ligonier Ministries.

thought of babies and adoption, we reminded ourselves that God was planning our lives. This was his problem, not ours. Does God have any problems? No, just solutions and purposes, I suspect. Needless to say, this was especially hard for me, a type-A control freak. Interestingly, the more John and I let go of the driver's seat of adoption searches and let God take control, the more he helped us get to a peaceful, contented, even enjoyable mindset—back to thriving and not just surviving. I believe God gave us this contentment because we backed off trying to control things and focused on his plan for us. "I am the LORD your God, who teaches you what is best for you, who directs you in the way you should go" (Isa. 48:17). I love, love, love that I don't have to figure it all out because, honestly, I'd have mountains of trouble trying to.

When all the trauma of infertility finally ceased, I felt cheery.

"That's funny, Cindy," John said when I told him, "because my hair's on fire with all the cheery we are doing."

We both belly-laughed until we cried. *Thank you, God, no more turmoil.* I was now loving these airy, fresh, free-flowing, sunny conversations and planning how to celebrate my birthday. This birthday was a special one for me, not because I'd reached a new decade but because we were free to be feather-brained, whimsical, and spirited again. I wanted something spectacular, a real flash with loads of creamy, dreamy chocolate and crusty bread and butter— real butter, not that fake stuff that's supposed to resemble butter but never comes near the real deal. We could dress up in bright, colorful, summer-island wear and have big flowers—an island assortment of flowers—to line the driveway and light the whole yard with tiki torches. Simply dreamy, I thought to myself.

That's the way you move your mind from pity to party, white-knuckling to surrendering with bright-heartedness. Meanwhile, Peaches was over at the neighbor's little makeshift garden eating all their tomatoes. Her whole face was covered in smashed tomato gunk, and our bellies hurt from laughing.

Together, we preached to ourselves this truth daily: we can't make it happen; only God can. We were training ourselves in contentment and being thankful for what we did have every single day. That's exactly what the apostle Paul said about how to train yourself to be settled and to thrive. We began giving our desires to God and finding ourselves increasingly freed from becoming too tangled in the crazy I-must-have-it web. I read in the Bible that "godliness with contentment is great gain" (1 Tim. 6:6). There's something about contentment, how helpful and hopeful it is, and I wanted great gain. Did we still want a child? A 100 percent *yes*, but not so desperately anymore. We took the focus off ourselves and put the burden on God, the only one who knew what was best for us. That diminished our craving.

In the book of Luke, God describes what it's like from his point of view when we ask him for things. He compares his desire to give his children good gifts to our desire to give good gifts. We all want to lavish our kids with the best gifts, don't we? I have a friend who starts Christmas shopping for her grandchildren in October. You should see her. She gets the best deals ever, like three electric scooters that originally sold for $60 for $15, a $119 electric shoe wheel for $19, and a princess bike for $20 reduced from $60. It makes you want to get out there and shop right now, doesn't it? That's what we do for our kids. Of course, God's gifts far exceed ours; they're heavenly gifts. Here's what God says:

> *Which of you fathers, if your son asks for a fish, will give him a snake instead? Or if he asks for an egg, will give him a scorpion? If you then, though you are evil, know how to give good gifts to your children, how much more will your Father in heaven give the Holy Spirit to those who ask him!*
>
> —Luke 11:11–13

Just like human parents, God never gives his children a bad gift. Let's take a quick look at the Holy Spirit, this gift from God. The Holy Spirit is our source of revelation, wisdom, and power. He's our helper and teaches and reminds us. He guides us to all truth, including knowledge of what is to come. He gives spiritual gifts to us. He intercedes for us when we are weak. And there is so much more. Pretty incredible gift, wouldn't you say?

Lord God, please help me remember these facts when I'm so stuck and don't really believe. Show me your better yes. Give me eyes, God, to see your goodness and to be grateful right where I am.

I once read a book on the life of Corrie ten Boom, who was imprisoned in a concentration camp during World War II. She was thankful for every moment, even in her horrendous conditions such as dreadful lice in her cell. Why? Because then the guards would not bother her. She would take a blade of grass from the yard, and when the officers marched her inside, she would enjoy it as if it were a bouquet of flowers in her cell. Now that's gratefulness.

CHAPTER FOUR

The Unbelievable Twist

Our anxiety does not empty tomorrow of its sorrows,
but only empties today of its strengths.
—Charles Spurgeon

We were living life large and feeling like newlyweds again. You know, we kind of skipped that season of our life. It had been sixth months since the drama of infertility, and I was ready for a new, lively experience—something captivating and interesting. So I mentioned it to John to see what he had to say.

"Let me run this thought by you," I said. "Kerry called and wants us to come with them to Cannes in Southern France. She wants us to go to their French villa."

"Let's go!" he said. "It could be a trip of a lifetime. We'll be living their jet-set lifestyle for 10 days. I say it would be a dream come true. We deserve it. Let's splurge."

"I agree. This is a trip of a lifetime."

We met Ray and Kerry, our British friends, on a cruise a few years before. We always enjoyed their company. It would be quite an adventure and surely a marvelously superb time.

They were thrilled that we said yes. Ray sent us keys and directions (in French) to their villa that sits in the rocky cliffs overlooking the Mediterranean Sea. And we were on our way. On the plane, a hefty man in the seat next to me snored the entire 15-hour flight to France. I didn't sleep a wink, so when we landed, all I wanted was to lie down for some much-needed zzz's. We hopped in a cab with the directions to Ray's villa, and off we went along the beach side of the French Riviera. What a sparkling morning by the sea! The sun was just beginning to glisten on the tiny waves crashing on the shore.

"Honey," John said, "we should try to get on the French time zone. Let's grab breakfast nearby."

My only meal had been that terrible chicken teriyaki in a mini tray on the airplane. Why do all the airlines serve chicken teriyaki? "I'm starved. How about you?" My stomach was grumbling like two pieces of sandpaper scraping each other. I couldn't decide what I wanted more, food or sleep. John tipped the cab driver while I grabbed my coat and purse out of the back seat. What a beautiful villa complex and view of the Riviera. Toto, we are not in Kansas anymore, I thought.

Since our friends would not arrive until evening, we decided to push through our complete exhaustion and walk down the hillside to a market we saw on our drive, the one overlooking the beach. It was a perfect spot for breakfast.

"Don't look now, honey, but it's George Clooney at the table behind you."

"Really?" I said, turning my head to see. Cannes is where the International Film Festival takes place, so it's not uncommon to see popular actors at the local restaurants. Many actors even have villas and homes in Cannes.

"Darn! False alarm. Just a look-alike," John said.

After our very French breakfast of baguettes and delicious pastries with jam and whipped cream, we headed back to grab a quick nap before our friends arrived that evening. It was delightful to see Kerry and Ray. It had been a few years since we'd been together. We reminisced until the wee hours of the morning on our lanai overlooking the Riviera, losing all track of time. We decided to hit the hay and resume tomorrow. We had so many stories to catch up on. We had always enjoyed our time together since that first meeting while sunning on the cruise ship deck.

I could hardly get up in the morning.

"Honey, we'd better get moving," John said.

"This bed is the most comfortable one I've ever snuggled in. I don't want to get up."

"Me neither, but Ray planned our yachting trip on his boat to Saint-Tropez today. You know, I've heard that's where all the movie stars go for holiday."

We loaded up in Ray and Kerry's Porsche and headed for the Cannes marina where their yacht was moored.

"My captain is ill and not available," Ray said, "but it's a quick trip, so I will captain." I felt a little uneasy as Ray didn't know exactly how to read the navigation maps that let you know where the shallow waters are or what buoys to follow out of harbors, among other things. Having grown up on the water with charts like these, I knew from Dad the importance of navigation.

Ray felt comfortable captaining, so my options were to either go with it and trust him or fake sickness. I decided to join them. How could I miss such a great adventure as Saint-Tropez?

I told John my uneasy feelings about Ray captaining, but he assured me. "He must know what he's doing," he said. "He owns the boat, after all." True. I decided to let go and enjoy the experience. Ray putt-putted out of the harbor. It was tricky navigation with so many boats harboring in this popular yacht club. Once we got out into open waters, he took off at supersonic speed. Tears literally flew out of my eyes. Then he came to a sudden stop in the middle of the Riviera.

"Honey, did you hear Ray?" I said. "We've run out of gas, and we're in the middle of the Mediterranean Sea."

We survived with the help of a local who gave us directions to the nearest island gas pump. Nevertheless, we had a sensational time sunning and swimming in the unimaginably beautiful crystal waters of the Mediterranean.

That evening we went to a truly luxurious hotel for dinner. "What a majestic hotel, Kerry, and what a spectacular view of the Riviera. It's a gorgeous place for dinner, if I do say so myself. It's such a beautiful evening. I didn't even bring my sweater."

"I know," said Kerry. "This time of year is so temperate. The thing is, Cindy, all the countries surrounding us come for holiday this time of year, so we have to book reservations early."

"Thank you so much for all this, Kerry."

The menu was extensive and unusual and, frankly, unappetizing. I knew France was supposed to be a food capital of the world, but fish served with the head on, seafood stew with prawn eyes staring at you and tentacles hanging out of the rice, and pasta topped in raw eggs weren't exactly appetizing foods to me. I felt weirdly nauseated but chalked it up to a change in environment and bizarre foods.

"What do you suggest for dinner?" I asked Kerry. "Do you have a favorite here?"

"I always order the same thing, prawns with drawn garlic butter and angel hair pasta simmering in white wine truffle olive oil with a Caprese side salad."

That sounded palatable to me, so I ordered the same thing. John had a large trout blackened over a grill served with a Romano parmesan polenta. Yes, the waiter delivered his fish with the head on—ugh!

Ray and Kerry's villa was set in the hills overlooking King Hussein's summer home on the French Riviera. Interestingly, the king was in. Guards were walking around the compound. What was that smell? I recognized it—curry. Of course it was curry, not the most pleasant aroma on this beautiful night. My stomach moaned. John and I sat together on our spacious lanai and watched the movement of the guards. We were fascinated—Americans who know nothing about kings and guards on compounds. We assumed the huge double fans blowing curry our way must have been from the king's kitchen. The curry did not help my stomach, for I was feeling uncomfortably nauseous by that time. I suggested to John that we head in for the night. It was getting late anyway. He agreed. I closed the door to our room and went to bed, hoping sleep would curtail my desire to vomit.

We enjoyed such unique, enchanting experiences in France and appreciated having a lavishly extravagant vacation. But even though we'd had many exciting adventures, I was getting anxious to be home, ready for my own bed. Ten days of travel and sleeping on different mattresses made me long for the creature comforts of my own—and my unusual queasiness was becoming a worry for me.

Once we were home, I still felt nauseated. Why? I was never nauseated. Something must be wrong. Maybe I'd had too much travel or caught the flu. There's always some bug on those flights. That must be it. My grandma used to give us kids Sprite for nausea. Maybe I should pick some up.

"Honey, you know me. I'm never queasy, ever." I mentioned this to John, hoping for some reassuring words. Then out of the blue, a thought occurred to me. Sitting at the end of my bed, I wondered if I could possibly be pregnant. What a strange thing to think. I'd been told by two very qualified physicians who actually saw inside my body cavity that I had no eggs and could not become pregnant. It was crazy to even speculate, yet I mentioned it to John.

"What? It's impossible for you to be pregnant," John said. "The surgery you had confirmed the fact that all your eggs are gone. Dr. Jarrett settled all of this."

"I know that, but I'm so nauseated for no good reason. I feel bloated and haven't had my period in two months, and I have no other symptoms of sickness."

"Okay, I hear you. Let's get a pregnancy test kit." He was trying to appease my crazy thoughts. We had to use the morning's first urine, so John suggested we relax. "You know it's impossible for you to be pregnant," he said again. "Remember, Dr. Jarrett actually went in with a camera. We have a movie of it somewhere."

"Honey, I do not want to see a movie of my insides. I told you that I'm queasy."

I tossed and turned all night before waking early to take my urine. The test turned blue.

"John," I said, shocked, "it's blue. Blue means pregnant. Look at this. It's blue."

"Maybe it's because of your medicines, Cindy. I don't know."

I immediately called Dr. Jones, my gynecologist, and gave him the pregnancy test results.

"It's impossible for you to be pregnant," he said. "It must be the hormone replacement drugs you're on that are giving you a false positive."

"But I've been so nauseous and bloated, and I haven't had my period in two months."

"Come in on Monday," he said, "and we will do an ultrasound to confirm no pregnancy, okay?"

"Okay, Dr. Jones."

I told John not to bother coming; it was just a formality. How could I ever be pregnant? He agreed. I went in on Monday, by myself. Why was I going through this formality when pregnancy was determinedly not possible? As I waited, draped in the green exam gown on the exam table, I felt sadness, anguish, and grief coming over me. Poor me, having to be tortured by going through with an ultrasound, pretending I might be pregnant. It wasn't fair. I don't deserve to be dealing with an impossible diagnosis. *Lord God, what are you doing here? Why am I going through these steps?*

As I lay on the table, the technician rolled the ultrasound probe around my belly. To my shock, she showed a real, live baby growing in my womb. A miracle! God's done this. Astonished, I wanted to jump off the table and shout to the sky, "Hallelujah! God has done a wonderful thing. I'm pregnant! It's God's work. He's done this for me!" I was vibrating. I was so ecstatic. I couldn't contain my excitement.

"Are you sure?" I asked the technician.

"Honey, of course I'm sure. You saw with your own eyes."

I did. It was just so impossible. "Thank you, Miss Harper."

"Don't thank me. I just showed you the sonogram."

I wanted to scream at the top of my lungs until all the air in me was gone. *Thank you, thank you, thank you, God!*

> *Many, LORD my God,*
> *are the wonders you have done,*
> *the things you have planned for us.*
> *None can compare with you;*
> *were I to speak and tell of your deeds,*
> *they would be too many to declare.*
> —Ps. 40:5

It was unbelievable. How long I had bent over backward to accomplish this, begging God and going through all those charts and needles and surgeries. Then out of nowhere, I was pregnant. Wow, wow, wow! How can I tell John? He's going to go crazy. I wonder what his first words will be. Will he scream like I want to? I'm sure he will. I can just picture him. I must get off this table to call him. When can I get off this table?

Dr. Jones entered the room. "Cindy, according to my calculations, you're two months pregnant. The baby's head and body are already visible." Wait until John hears two months pregnant and can see our baby's head and body. Suddenly, though, like day turning to night, it became clear to me that Dr. Jones wasn't sharing my excitement. His next words shocked me. "You need to abort the baby."

Uh, what? Was he talking about my miracle baby, the one I had strived for so many difficult years to have, the one God had clearly given to me against impossible odds?

He explained that there was a one-in-four chance our child would be deformed. I don't remember why. It may have been because of the medicine I was taking for menopause. I had started hormone replacement immediately after finding out I was in menopause, the same day I had surgery and found out I couldn't have children and discovered that all my eggs were gone. I was way too young to be naturally in menopause, so maybe that was the problem. I don't know. I don't remember all the intricacies of what was going on because all I could think was this: *How could this doctor be saying abort? Doesn't he know how long I have waited for this pregnancy? How long I prayed for a child? Doesn't he realize God has brought this miracle child to me?* I needed to get out of there. I couldn't process what he was saying. I rejected his words. It would be the last time I would trust what doctors said over what I knew in my heart was right.

The minute I left, I called John and blurted out these words: "Honey, I'm pregnant!" I had thought about saying those words for what seemed like an eternity. Through all my infertility, they sounded heavenly to my aching ears. I wish I had set him up more, like, "Honey, guess what news I have?" and take him through a series of questions for him to guess. John had to sit down to grasp this incomprehensible news.

Everyone knew about our infertility problems, so this news was completely astonishing. We spent most of the day celebrating, literally dancing around at this gift, this impossible gift, with every person who knew our story—friends, family, coworkers. It was a miracle. "The LORD has done this, and it is marvelous in our eyes" (Ps. 118:23).

No truer words were ever penned.

John and I were on cloud nine. After all those fertility charts and procedures and searches, after all the endless work and striving that showed John and me how incapable we were to produce a child, God had done the impossible for us. After all that emotional turmoil and heartache, boom! In a nanosecond, it was all redeemed. All the horrible, endless pursuing that ended in nothing had now been completely reversed. God had just answered our very deep, personal heart's desire. I hadn't even been praying for it anymore. But our heavenly Father knew. Oh, how he cares for me. I was seeing his love for me personally, his tender compassion, and his nearness.

I had strived and manipulated and controlled my circumstances ad nauseam trying to have a child. When I finally gave up, I threw my hands in the air and started to accept the way things were. I began to relax in what *was* and not what I *wanted*. The intense feeling of I-must-have-a-baby lessened.

"Take delight in the Lord, and he will give you the desires of your heart" (Ps. 37:4). As I delight in God, he is in the business of my heart's desires. *God, I'm trying to believe in such a way that I can delight in you.* As I read that verse again and again, it finally jumped out to me. My trust and faith, my belief, will let me delight in God. As I get to know him, the one who richly gives us all we need for our enjoyment, delight and heart desires follow. I'm all about that. My new understanding initiated a slow simmering into my soul through all my adversity. Scripture does say that God is speaking to us in our afflictions. This must have been it.

It was month four of my baby's growth and time for another ultrasound. I had weekly appointments because I was considered high-risk. I didn't mind. I enjoyed every ultrasound. Baby Jonathan (yes, we were having a boy) would put on great shows for all to see. He would do flips and suck his thumb. He looked perfectly beautiful. We could see his facial features and count all his little toes and fingers. Just hearing his heartbeat was amazing to me. Spending time at the ultrasound with him made it feel like he was already born. What a special gift! I wondered what he would do at each checkup. He was quite a show-off. Between flips and sucking his thumb, we never knew what else he'd perform. I'm so grateful for such clear machines that allowed me to actually see inside my body, to see my baby boy, my perfect boy.

Bob and Jane, our neighbors with the garden where our escape artist Peaches gorges her fat self on juicy ripe tomatoes, were like parents to us, and I knew they'd want to experience a baby ultrasound. Although they had 10 grandkids, they had not seen a single ultrasound, so I invited them to come along with me. Why not? I wanted everyone to meet Jonathan.

We all gathered in the ultrasound room and watched as the technician started to move the probe up my belly. We listened intently as she explained everything we could see. Out of the blue, Bob asked if he could see an enlargement of the heart. *That's a weird request*, I thought. The technician enlarged the image of Jonathan's heart and paused. Something caught her eye.

"What's wrong?" I asked.

She said calmly that she thought she saw an abnormality but couldn't be sure. She didn't say much more, only that she was making an appointment that afternoon with the hospital for a special Doppler ultrasound that could show the blood flowing through Jonathan's heart.

That was strange and a little unnerving. I got off the table, feeling uneasy. I asked if everything was okay with Jonathan. She reassured me that whatever it was, the Doppler people would get to the bottom of it. I had been walking with God long enough to know that there are no coincidences in life, only God directing circumstances. So I bowed my head. *You are in charge, God, of Jonathan and me. After all, you gave me my miracle baby. Please keep my thoughts on straight and don't let those fear-and-worry beasts out of their cages. Please, God, they are beating at the door. Thank you for Bob and Jane being here; they are like grandparents to me, as you know. God, I'm reminding myself that this is your plan. Amen.*

I didn't want to scare John at work or interrupt his day, so I didn't call him. I had a bad feeling about it, almost as if God were preparing me in advance for something not good. The circumstances were too familiar, reminding me of when I'd brought my friend along to my doctor's appointment and found the grapefruit-sized tumor in my chest. How can this be? *Jonathan is your miracle child, God.* I tried to shrug off the feelings. The Clarks and I went for a quick lunch before my scheduled Doppler ultrasound. I stewed the entire time, reliving how this was not going to be good. Bob and Jane tried to comfort me, but it just wasn't happening. The more I thought, the more anxious I became.

We arrived at the community hospital right at 2:00 p.m. and followed the yellow brick road, hospital-style, to our ultrasound room. The tech was calling my name as we walked in. I climbed on the sonogram table and got comfortable. With at least five doctors and Bob and Jane standing behind me, I wished I had called John. Something was not right because he wasn't there to hold my hand and be part of this thing going on with his son. What a terrible decision it was to not call him. Ugh! The technician darkened our room, and my tears started flowing. The doctors were throwing around a lot of scientific talk. Some of it I could understand from my science background, but for lots of it, I had no idea. What was evident to all was their concern. I knew it wasn't good.

After the doctors finished, I was escorted into a hospital room alone. The room had floor-to-ceiling windows on one wall. I stared out at all the gray outside, my eyes searching for and wanting to find some glimmer of color, some escape from what was about to come down. Not seeing a flicker of rosy color, I turned frantically, pacing. *Where is John? What am I doing all alone at this critical hour? How did I get here?* My heart raced. The beasts were now free. I felt like a caged rat wanting to claw out. Finally, a white-coat doctor came in. I could feel my adrenaline surging as he entered the room. He got right to the point, no introductions, for which I was glad. I would not have heard a word he said. He explained that Jonathan had a heart condition that would end his life in one to 14 days after his birth. The news was shattering and so emotionally devastating that I became ill. My world stopped. I couldn't believe it. It made no sense. Jonathan was my miracle baby from God himself. Now he was going to die? What? How could that be? He was from the Lord. God had given me my miracle. There was no way he would take it back. Impossible!

What about all those Bible verses, God, about you giving me my heart's desire? You then deliver to me my greatest longing only to take him away from me. No! No! No! How can you do this to me? I burned with anger. I did not have a box big enough for the emotion in me. I'd never felt it before. I simply did not know this God who would pull the rug right out from under my feet and take my baby away. I had put all my eggs, my hopes, in the God basket. How could he ever devastate me like this? How could I tell John? What do I tell John? I didn't even call him to give him a chance to be part of this. I'm wrecked.

I made a quick call to John. My pain level was so off the charts that I cared little about how he might feel, I'm very sad to say. I told him there was a problem with Jonathan and to please come to the hospital. "Bob and Jane are with me," I said, and hung up. John arrived at the hospital in record time, a solid 30 minutes. After seeing my face, he knew it was grave. All I could say was it's about his heart, and we walked into the conference room where the physicians were waiting. We pleaded with them to please save Jonathan. A heart transplant was the only option they offered, but it was extremely risky. The doctors were dismal about Jonathan's future if he had a transplant.

We also were told that they would not perform the surgery if Jonathan was born without a spleen or if his organs were flipped. Apparently, it's quite common to have flipped organs, but attaching tiny arteries and veins is quite impossible when that is the case. The doctors were 98 percent sure of their diagnosis.

Our walk to the car that bleak afternoon felt like an eternity. The cold grayness on my face penetrated deep into my now-cemented heart. I stared out the window, my faced pressed against the cold glass as cars sped by. I tried to gather my thoughts, but it was no use. I felt numb and lifeless, wishing the world would end or I could at least jump off. We didn't speak a word all the way home. What was left to say? Honey, how are you doing? No, we already knew how we were doing. We were hurting; we were hopeless. This was supposed to be our time, our big reveal, our future happiness, all our dreams coming true.

I opened the door to our house and dragged myself in, wanting to give up and escape this life-altering, horrendous news. I wanted to pretend, like children do, that it wasn't real. I wanted to pull the blankie over my head. I wanted to say "uncle" to God—you win, I give up, I can't do it anymore, take me home. I went to our room, crawled into bed, and bawled my eyes out. I told Jonathan that I was going to take care of him; I was going to protect him. "Sweetie, I'm not going to let anything happen to you. Momma loves you, baby boy. She will watch over you." The physicians said that while he was in my womb, my body would help with his blood supply. He was secure. But when he was born and I'd no longer be helping his blood flow, everything would change. John lay next to me, and we both held Jonathan with our hands on my belly.

We had a very short time to decide about whether to do a heart transplant. One morning very early, during our best thinking time, we sat down together in our favorite sitting chairs off the kitchen and prayed. We discussed Jonathan's options, knowing there was a team of surgeons waiting to meet with us. Our biggest prayer was "God, don't make us decide this, please." Frankly, there was not much to talk about. God, through the surgeons, would have to decide. What did John and I know about all this technical medical jargon anyway? We met with our team of doctors who told us what to expect from a transplant. It was all so much to take in. We kept praying that God would not make us make this serious decision. Fervently we prayed, "God, please, take this decision out of our hands. Heal Jonathan."

God had been helping me heal from the sharp, penetrating wounds he inflicted through Jonathan's diagnosis. Slowly, the God I knew was rising out of my ash heap to his rightful position. I always knew the truth in my heart. I was just so mad. He was reminding me that he hadn't left me. I knew my story was not finished, so I bowed my head and continued forward with him in the driver's seat, his rightful place. It was the only option. In the book of Jonah in the Bible, Jonah gets eaten by a large fish. It's a true story; it says God provided a huge fish to swallow Jonah (Jon. 1:17). Why? Because Jonah did not like God's plan. Jonah lived three days in that fish. God then had the huge fish spit him out. Jonah learned a lot of wonderful, life-changing things about God during that time. I was learning a lot about God, too. We knew God would answer our prayers immeasurably more than we could ask or imagine because we believed what the Bible says in Ephesians 3:20. We remembered Elijah, a human being just like us, who "prayed earnestly that it would not rain, and it did not rain on the land for three and a half years" (James 5:17). If God would answer Elijah's dramatic prayer for no rain, why wouldn't he answer our prayer in the same way?

Our parents wanted us to have an abortion, and understandably so. "How can you carry a baby to term knowing he's going to die?" they said. They loved us and didn't want us to suffer. We considered this as an option. I kept thinking about all the time I had spent with Jonathan at my ultrasound appointments, about my promise to take care of him, about how real he was. I had seen him suck his thumb and do flips, and I'd counted his tiny fingers and toes. He was real in there—my baby. How could I consider killing him? But he was going to die anyway if we didn't do the transplant. *Oh, God, help me! I cannot think this way clearly.* Then I found this passage in the Bible:

> *You have searched me, LORD,*
> *and you know me.*
> *You know when I sit and when I rise;*
> *you perceive my thoughts from afar.*

You discern my going out and my lying down;
    you are familiar with all my ways.
For you created my inmost being;
    you knit me together in my mother's womb.
I praise you because I am fearfully and wonderfully made;
    your works are wonderful,
    I know that full well.
My frame was not hidden from you
    when I was made in the secret place,
    when I was woven together in the depths of the earth.
Your eyes saw my unformed body;
    all the days ordained for me were written in your book
    before one of them came to be.

—Ps. 139:1–3, 13–16

God was showing me his detailed involvement and care. See how much he's in the intricate moments of our lives, how carefully he's watching over us and how tenderly he's providing? God was showing John and me that he knew, that he is the architecture of everything about Jonathan and about us. He was completely protecting all of us. There was nowhere he was not. His strong hand was holding us, and he was the one who had created every cell of our bodies and knit Jonathan in my womb. All of this work was too wonderful for us to comprehend with our earthly, human minds. Jonathan was created by God in my womb for God's good, wonderful, loving purposes for him, John, and me. God's eyes saw that Jonathan's body was exactly how it was meant to be. It was not imperfect as the world might think; it was most perfect, just as God wanted. All Jonathan's days had been written in God's book way before he was created. How comforting to know that as we approached the difficult road of his potential death.

It was painful to know that I couldn't control what was going on, but what an incomparable comfort to know that God had my son in his arms through the whole ordeal. John and I couldn't see the next steps we needed to take or where they would eventually take us, but we knew that God did, and that knowledge gave us hope and strength to proceed and face whatever God had next.

We spoke with the team of physicians about Jonathan's potential heart transplant, and they answered all our questions so we could make our very difficult decision.

"Our most pressing question is Jonathan's quality of life," John said. "Can you tell us about that?"

The doctor explained it this way: Jonathan will have to be on substantial, strong antirejection drugs to keep his body from refusing the new heart. These medicines, while good for what they do, have many side effects. These are lifelong side effects that wreak havoc on his body. He will have to be careful around other children so he doesn't catch common viruses. His body could not tolerate them. He will be in and out of hospitals yearly. Even if everything goes perfectly, he will still live as a sickly child.

We had learned some of that in our extensive research about heart transplants, and we were aware that Jonathan would have a very difficult life with lots of pain and suffering. Based on all the knowledge we'd gathered, we decided against having a transplant. You'd think you would do anything to spare your child's life, but when confronted with the thought of your child suffering, you find you make different decisions.

We experienced great anguish over this choice, and we continued begging God to spare us from it and save Jonathan. It's an impossible decision for parents to make. We could not understand why God had us in this crucible. It wasn't right, and it was painful and wearisome. I cannot write adequately the burden it was to come to a verdict. We asked God to help us trust that Jonathan's outcome was still under his control. We took comfort in that prayer, and together we bowed our heads in faith and moved forward, one step at a time. Though we continued daily to plead for God's intervention, we knew that, ultimately, Jonathan's life was in God's hands. It was his decision.

We decided that I would carry Jonathan to term and claimed this verse from the Lord: "We can make our plans, but the LORD determines our steps" (Prov. 16:9 NLT).

Jonathan was flourishing in my womb. I was as big as a house. We learned that Jonathan's exact diagnosis was hypoplastic left heart syndrome, which means he had three chambers in his heart instead of four. Knowing that inside my womb I was helping his blood flow and that he was completely healthy was such an encouragement to me. I could protect my son in my womb from the terrible harm that would come to him when he was born. I didn't want him to come out. He was so active in my womb, rolling back and forth. I knew he was complete and happy in there.

I first felt Jonathan move inside me when John and I were on a Caribbean cruise, sunning on the ship's deck. It was a beautiful day. Suddenly, Jonathan literally rolled from one side of my belly to the other. His hand or foot stuck out.

"Did you see that, John?"

"What?"

Then he rolled again. This time, John saw him. We forgot all about Jonathan's prognosis and enjoyed pregnancy as normal people do. What an exhilarating, fun, lighthearted vacation. *Thank you, God.* We felt as if God had us in the eye of a hurricane for a brief moment, a place where it's calm and sunny. What a wonderful reprieve!

Even when difficult moments came in my pregnancy, God gave me what can only be described as a supernatural calm. "And the peace of God, which transcends all understanding, will guard your hearts and your minds in Christ Jesus" (Phil. 4:7). His peace was guarding my heart and my mind.

I was a real estate agent in my city, and I loved my job. It was like being back at college all over again. The agents at our office were like family, and we so enjoyed one another's company. Everyone in my office knew my condition, but the clients weren't aware, so they inevitably asked the normal questions: When are you due? Do you know what you're having? Some would ask very detailed questions. What color is the baby's room? What is the theme for the nursery? Those were the hardest because I didn't decorate Jonathan's room or have a baby shower to gather things for him. I fully believed God was going to heal him, yet I did very little to prepare for his care after birth. I can't tell you why. But when those questions came up, what was I to say? How could I tell everyone my baby was expected to die? It would have been so awkward for all in earshot of it.

It would have been natural for me to fall to pieces every time I was faced with all that questioning, but God kept me calm and peaceful and gave me his supernatural ability to handle these situations. I never melted into a puddle, not even once. Sometimes I felt a little awkward but only because I worried about making others feel awkward. *Thank you, God, for giving me words to answer all the incoming curiosity. I'm so grateful, Lord, that this is so enjoyable for me. It sounds crazy to even say that. It has to be you giving it to me. Father, this is what I asked you for so many moons ago—that I could be big and fat and pregnant with my own baby rolling around in my tummy. Pure ecstasy. Thank you for answering my prayer. It reminds me of Dad's Alzheimer's disease and how you gave him and me such a beautiful, wonderful season together against everything expected.*

I'm here to tell you I did not and still do not have adequate faith or emotional strength to withstand questions about my dying son. Only God could give me the confidence to handle the road he had me on. My natural tendency is to worry, and I have a bent toward negativity. But God put this happiness in me. I could not be calm any other way. It was simply impossible. This calm is what the Bible describes—it's supernatural from God, no *me* in it at all.

I thoroughly enjoyed my pregnancy. While the doctors were 98 percent sure of Jonathan's diagnosis, I believed 100 percent that God would heal him. The Bible says in Hebrews that faith is sure and certain, although we can't see it. It's as if it's already done. Hebrews 11:1 says, "Now faith is confidence in what we hope for and assurance about what we do not see." Some friends thought I was in denial, but I was really living on faith.

I knew that nothing pleases God more than my belief in him and his abilities. Hebrews 11:6 says that "without faith it is impossible to please God." Often I heard others say that Jonathan would be healed if it was God's will. Obvious as that was, I would tell them that as a mother, the only prayer I had in me was for my son's healing. I'm sure and certain of this: God was pleased with my faith. Anytime we are all-in with our heartfelt prayers, God is pleased, so pleased. In Matthew 21:21, Jesus says, "Truly I tell you, if you have faith and do not doubt, not only can you do what was done to the fig tree, but also you can say to this mountain, 'Go throw yourself into the sea,' and it will be done." Pray what you can, and leave all of it to God.

We decided to have Jonathan by C-section to give him every opportunity for life. The stress of labor and going through the birth canal would have been difficult for him. A plan was set; we would have him on June 2 at a hospital equipped with specific care for his needs. It had underground tunnels connecting to a prominent pediatric hospital. Jonathan could be born at one place and then whisked away to the critical care specialists at the other hospital. It was a brilliant plan.

We arrived early in the morning. One of our favorite pastors, David, came from our home-away-from-home church. That's what I called our church because it had become an extended family for John and me. David was gentle and kind; his eyes evidenced his compassion. He was someone people wanted a stone's throw away when things got tough. His deep, soft voice was like your grandfather's. He began praying those beautiful, comforting, hope-filled words of God, and I knew then it was all going to be okay. "Today is D-day, baby Jonathan. God is going to have to pump blood from your tiny heart to the rest of your perfect body." Most of my nerves were because Jonathan would no longer be able to use my body to help pump his blood.

Oh, how I really didn't want him to come out. I knew he was so safe inside of me. I was traumatized by how much he would struggle without my blood flowing through his tiny veins. The thought of his struggle haunted me. I wanted to holler, "Stop! Don't let him out! What on earth could I do to keep him in?! How will I be able to protect him anymore?"

The time had arrived, and John and I entered the birthing room. Dr. Denny had his naturally bright smile on. Man, that guy had the most beautiful teeth. He was allegedly one of the most sought-after eligible bachelors in town. The nurses went crazy at the mention of Dr. Denny. He administered my epidural, and we were able to watch the entire process with fascination. After much pulling—you'd be amazed at how much physical strength is required to deliver a baby—Jonathan finally came out. He was as beautiful as a doll. He looked like the healthiest newborn I'd ever seen, more than eight pounds and rosy. He had a perfectly symmetrical round head, chubby cheeks, strong features, and a cute pug nose. He looked more like a three-month-old than a freshly born baby. C-section babies, I've been told, are beautiful because they don't have to push through the birth canal. That makes sense to me.

John and I got to hold him and finally touch his darling face, the one I'd seen on computer monitors for so many months. "Baby Jonathan, it's your mom and dad," I said. It was pure satisfaction, such an unexpected pleasure beyond any natural feeling I've ever experienced. I relished the moment, savoring every touch of his skin. I wished with everything in me that this moment in time would stand still forever. It was magical. I didn't want it to end.

After checking Jonathan over and making him comfortable, the pediatric specialist and his team took him through the underground tunnel to the pediatric hospital. John went with them, but I had to stay in post-op to stabilize after surgery. I was feeling pretty euphoric from the morphine drip, which took away the excruciating pain I should be feeling. It also helped me emotionally, taking the grief edge away as painkillers often do. The news came back pretty quickly. Jonathan was born just as the doctors had said he would be, with hypoplastic left heart syndrome. Oddly, I was not devastated, thanks to my morphine drip and mostly to God, who had been taking care of my emotions all along. He was there with me. I thought I would have been more heartbroken since I had fully believed that Jonathan would be whole and healed. Some would say because I believed God would heal him against 98 percent odds, I had left myself open to much hurt, that I wasn't being truthful with the facts and my feelings about those facts. The truth is that God gave me grace and mercy and comfort to deal with this news. It was just like him to bathe me in comfort after I had believed in him to do mighty things. As the verse says, with faith, we can move mountains and tell fig trees to be thrown into the sea. This faith is what God wanted; he wanted me to believe him for mighty things. I always say this: Pray for the impossible, and you take care of the possible. You pray for sure and certain with that kind of belief.

It was warm and sunny that early June day when Jonathan was born. His doctors gave us much freedom with him. You'd think he'd be in the neonatal intensive care unit (NICU), but we had total, do-whatever-you-like protocol. Probably because he was dying, they wanted us to have as much time with him as possible. Over the next few days, we took Jonathan outside into the grassy courtyard of the hospital. The sun shone on his face, glistening on his chubby cheeks and lighting up his eyes. He definitely had John's vibrantly blue eyes. He was beautiful, and everyone in the NICU said so.

"It's surreal that this little guy is the only one who's dying," I told John. "So many other babies on the NICU floor look so sick. Then there's Jonathan, who's twice their size, with perfect features and vibrant skin. He's vigorous, and he's the one who's going to die. I can hardly bear this agony, John."

"Me too, Cindy," John said solemnly. "Me too." When we'd see people in the hospital elevator or outside on the grounds, they would all say how beautiful Jonathan was. No one knew he was the baby who was dying.

One afternoon, I distinctly remember looking into Jonathan's bright eyes and noticing a void, an emptiness, as if he wasn't there. Today, I would explain it as the Alzheimer's look—those who know dear ones with this disease can understand immediately what I'm talking about. You know how people refer to the sparkle in children's eyes? Jonathan did not have a sparkle. He looked like a perfectly beautiful porcelain doll, but he had a blank stare. There was never any interaction. It was as if God had already taken him home to heaven. Looking back, perhaps God was protecting our hearts with his healing balm already.

John was stressed about it. "I'm so tense my skin is crawling, and my heart is pounding," he said. "I'd like to go run—20 miles. But I don't have it in me. I'm so concerned that he's suffering."

"I know, John. Can you tell if he's in pain?"

"His doctors say no."

"But he won't eat anything. I'm so exhausted just watching his every breath. I'm so tired and sore and sick and sad," I said.

"Me too, but not the sore part. Ha ha."

I pulled his arm around me. "Can you just hold me really tight and tell me it's going to be okay?"

"Of course," he said. "Let's not stop holding, okay?"

"Yes. Yes."

There was no indication that Jonathan was in any distress. He seemed content, but he refused any food. I grieved because I wanted him to do what babies are supposed to do—cry, eat, and poop. We asked the doctor to give Jonathan shots of morphine because we worried that he was in pain. The doctors reassured us that they didn't think he was suffering, yet at our request, Jonathan got a morphine injection. The doctors would do whatever we wanted for him. Again, I think it was to ease our pain. We all knew without words being said that his time was short.

All our friends came to see him and hold him. We sometimes had 30 people in our room at a time. Jonathan never lay in a crib; there were so many people wanting to hold him. Our good friend Terri took the night shift and held him all night. Even our doctors would hold him in the night. Having such a huge support system brought us a lot of reassurance and comfort, but by the third day, we were undone and in desperate need of alone time with Jonathan and some much-needed sleep. The doctors put a No Visitors sign up on our door.

John was with me in the hospital room all the time. The staff was wonderful and turned our room into a mini suite for the three of us. We didn't do a lot of talking. Being so overwhelmed with our emotions of grief and exhaustion just didn't leave room for dialogue. What could we say to each other, anyway? We mostly slept and rocked Jonathan as we waited for him to die. The doctors predicted that it would take up to two weeks.

On the morning of the fifth day, John said he was taking Jonathan for a morphine shot. As he left, I looked at the clock in my hospital room, and the Lord told me in my heart, clear as you are alive today, that it was over, that Jonathan had passed away. There was no immediate medical reason for this to be the end for Jonathan, yet God prepared me for the grief I would go through. John returned with tears in his eyes and Jonathan in his arms. I said, "I know. God told me." It was profoundly personal that the Lord God would prepare me for this news in advance. Sometimes just moments of notice are enough to brace you for what's next.

We left the hospital that day, exhausted and frazzled, worn out and beat down from caring for our very sick, dying child. I went home to bed, but John had to go to the funeral home to make arrangements. I was still too weak from the C-section to go along. I hadn't had a moment to recuperate. John said he would call when he got to the funeral home so we could talk about the details and the casket and make other decisions such as what to put in the casket with Jonathan. I was obsessed with what the inside of the casket should be like and what we were going to have in it. I wanted a soft, cozy, happy place for Jonathan to lay his head.

John could not comprehend that at all. He had no box for my irrational thoughts. He knew Jonathan was not there. I knew that, too. What did it matter? He was in heaven with Jesus. I knew that intellectually, but I was so stuck in my sorrow. I wanted my baby comfortable and happy—what every mom wants. John just wanted to get out of the funeral home. He knew Jonathan was going to be delivered to the funeral home from the hospital that day, and that fact weighed heavily on his heart. We argued. As I went round and round about what blanket and pacifier and rattle to place in his coffin, John got more irritated and angrier. It sounds crazy now, but my feelings were off the charts. The stress and grieving were taking their toll. I just couldn't let go of the details. *How comfy was the casket?* We ended in a stalemate, and John chose what he knew I'd cared most about before scooting out and heading home, feeling relieved that it was over.

The next order of business was to decide whether to have a funeral service. I was not interested in a viewing or a service. We both were emotionally spent, and I was still recovering. What was the point? Just more pain and suffering for us. And we would have to make conversation with a multitude of people. Remember our hospital room?

"It just seems unacceptable for us," I said. "I say no." But the more we thought about it, the more we realized this was not just about us. What about all the people who wanted to celebrate Jonathan? Wouldn't we want that, too? Yes, of course we'd want to share his life with others. I was just so weak and sore that I could not imagine standing for hours greeting and making conversation with hoards of people. Logistically, I just didn't know if I could do it. Maybe if I had a chair to rest in, that might work. My uneasiness began to dissipate as I contemplated having some relief if I needed it.

The next few days after Jonathan's death, I spent much of my time thinking about what it was like for him now. I wondered what he could be doing in heaven. Would the Lord be coddling him in his arms? I had no idea. Maybe. Jesus says, "Let the little children come to me, and do not hinder them, for the kingdom of heaven belongs to such as these" (Matt. 19:14). God knew Jonathan's heart's desires better than I ever could have as his mom.

I hadn't wanted him to be born because I knew I couldn't have control over him. Not that I ever had control; it just felt like I did. But I couldn't protect him any longer. Finally, after all those months of wondering how to make him safe in my belly and how to keep him safe when he came out, I knew that Jonathan was safe and healthy and at home. From what the Bible says about eternity, he must be having the time of his life in heaven. No crying, and all of his desires are constantly perfectly met. I could never do that down here on earth. I also knew he could never have had that life here on earth with me and John.

The Bible says so much about heaven. How exciting it was for me to read about Jonathan at home and, eventually, me at home. Heaven is described as a perfect, earthlike place where Jesus and the Father are and where there is no sin (Rev. 21:1–5). The streets are made of gold (Rev. 21:21). Think about that. What I consider beautiful and what makes me wealthy on earth is pavement for my feet to trample on in heaven. Jesus has built mansions and prepared a place for each of us (John 14:2). Imagine what that looks like. I hope mine will be on a beach because I love the ocean. Do you wonder where yours will be? Do you wonder what Jonathan's home is like?

Author Randy Alcorn is known for his perspective on heaven. The *Gospel Herald* wrote this about what he had to say in an article called "Randy Alcorn on Biblical View of Heaven: Will We Play Sports? What Age Will We Be?"

What age will we be in heaven?...Because passages in Isaiah mention children being in heaven (see Isaiah 11 and Isaiah 65), the author [Alcorn] believes that children who die prior to reaching their physical peak in life will be the same age that they were on earth. He believes that Jesus' words in the Sermon on the Mount could support the idea that such children get the chance to grow up in heaven (see Matthew 5). "You've experienced mourning, I will give you laughter. You were deprived of raising a child who died at a young age, maybe you will be able to be there with your child as he or she grows up on the new earth without threat of death, harm, abuse, or anything else," Alcorn says.[4]

Think about it: John and I may get to raise Jonathan in a perfect world—perfect, so no suffering. Now that's a thrilling thought. The article went on to say:

As for travelling, Alcorn says that the idea of leisurely vacationing in heaven is not too far-fetched. "The new earth will correspond to the old earth in the same way that our new bodies will correspond to our old bodies—a better version of the same—but not fundamentally different, except in the sense of [being] perfected," [Alcorn says].[5]

4. Lauren Leigh Noske, "Randy Alcorn on Biblical View of Heaven: Will We Play Sports? What Age Will We Be?" *The Gospel Herald*, https://www.gospelherald.com/articles/54763/20150317/randy-alcorn-on-heaven-will-we-play-sports-what-age-will-we-be.htm?gclid=EAIaIQob ChMIs7rgtP3o6AIVOvfjBx0ZbQE5EAAYASAAEgKHqfD_BwE.
5. Ibid.

Alcorn also believes "we will regularly feast in heaven, as the practice is mentioned in Scripture almost 200 times (see Matthew 8:11). 'Feasting involves celebration and fun; it's profoundly relational. Great conversation, storytelling, relationship-building, and laughter happen during mealtimes.'"[6]

This world is not our home. We are called foreigners and strangers here on earth (1 Pet. 2:11). We are all progressing toward the existence that comes after this one. I grieve with hope because Jonathan had the privilege of arriving in heaven a little bit earlier. He had to live only five days on what the Bible calls this sin-cursed earth, and then he got to go home to paradise with Jesus for the rest of his life. What more could a mother want for her son?

God, however, didn't just take Jonathan to his wonderful fate and not consider our pain and the pain of those who loved him as collateral damage. No, God works all things together for the good of those who love him (Rom. 8:28). All things. All His plans are good and perfect.

More than 300 people attended Jonathan's funeral. It was a true celebration of his birth and death into Jesus's arms. Many were moved by God's amazing grace to us during this difficult tragedy. John wrote this story of Jonathan's short life on earth.

From Jonathan's Eyes

The Life of Jonathan Jared Schmidler, 9:00 a.m., Monday, June 3, 1991–Friday, June 7, 1991, 9:55 a.m. "Jesus said, 'Let the little children come to me, and do not hinder them, for the kingdom of heaven belongs to such as these'" (Matt. 19:14).

---

6. Ibid.

June 3, 1991 – Prelude

Mom and Dad got up at 4:30 a.m. to get to the hospital by 6:00 a.m. so this story could unfold. I had no way of knowing that the place I had called home for 38 weeks would soon be invaded by a doctor. I could tell something was up because Mom felt awfully nervous, and Dad sounded uptight. I heard them say we were at IU Hospital, and that they were both afraid and lonely. Then they saw David our shepherding minister in the hallway of the labor delivery area, and a peace settled over both Mom and Dad. David came just at the right time, and the action was now getting close.

Day 1 – June 3, 1991
8:48 a.m.

I was born breech by C-section, which was a huge shock for me and lots of pain for Mom. Dad just sat and watched. The first guy I saw was Dr. Denny, whom I had heard many times, and it was great to associate a name with a face, even if I was upside down. He did a wonderful job with Mom and had to really work hard to get her back together. As they whisked me out of the operating room, the mood was all tense and professional—definitely all business. Everyone was worried I might not make it, so they had a whole staff of doctors and nurses working on me to wake me up. At 8:47, I was in a warm, comfortable womb, and by 8:49, I was on a table under lights with doctors trying to convince me to breathe. Well, they succeeded, because my work here on earth would not be done until Friday. And besides, I had not met my mom yet. When

I woke up, Dad, wearing a goofy hat and mask, was staring at me. Dad then left to check on Mom, and I met two special people who would be my friends my whole life—Dr. David and my nurse Caryn.

Dad came back and said Mom was doing real well. She hoped that I was 45 pounds, but to her amazement, I was only 7 pounds 7 ounces and 20 1/2 inches long.

Once they stabilized me, it was time for the big moment: I got to meet my mom. She was more beautiful than I ever expected, and now I know why I heard all those whistles (at least the first four months). I could now see the love in her eyes as well as feel it in my heart. Because everyone was concerned about my heart, the doctors felt it best to take me over to Riley Children's Hospital, which specializes in children with severe health problems. They typically would put me in a metal container for the trip, but Dr. David and Caryn pulled some strings and let Dad hold me while they pushed us in a wheelchair. Caryn pushed; Dr. David directed. What a team. Look out, Indy 500 fans.

The nursery in module 5 at Riley would be my home for tonight. My nurse was Sabine (she told me how her first name was of German origin and pronounced sa-BEAN-a). She took great care of me Monday. Dad was there the whole time; I think he forgot about Mom for a while. Sabine hooked me up to a heart and respiration monitor so they could keep track of me. I would set off the alarms on both units if anyone even tried to change my diaper. Dr. Darrell (my heart specialist) showed up around 11:00 with his ultrasound machine to check my heart. He felt I would have a tough time using my heart for a very long time because all the parts weren't in the right places. It happened during the time I was developing, but it in no way affected the room I had available for love.

Mom got wheeled over on her bed, and it was good to see her. I missed her. I'm so glad Michelle, Julie, Debbie, and Kim were with Mom, because I think Dad forgot about her. Next, I saw Grandma and Grandpa and Aunt Barbara. I was as excited to see them as they were to see me. It's great to have grandparents. They all held and rocked me. It was great.

Mom stayed until 4:30 and then got wheeled back to IU. She was tired. Lots of Mom and Dad's friends came to visit Mom at IU; Dad escorted each one to see me—he was truly a proud daddy. Even more of their friends called to check up on us. It was great. I slept at Riley that night, mostly in Sabine's arms. She said I was a model patient.

It was a good day.

Day 2 – June 4, 1991

I woke up early, and Sabine was rocking me, attempting to get me to eat some awful-tasting formula. Mom and Dad came over early. Mom was still in her bed.

As I looked around the intensive care unit, I saw all kinds of children who needed lots of help. I hope they all make it. I really didn't look like I should be there because my appearance on the outside was great. It was inside where the problems were. The doctors felt I wouldn't make it very long, but I'd show them.

I had lots of visitors today, all friends of Mom and Dad—and now of me. It was great to meet them and have them hold me. Grandma and Grandpa got here at 12:00 noon. It was exciting to meet them. It's great to have grandparents.

The doctors stopped giving me the medication, which was supposed to help my heart, at 1:30 p.m. They felt I would be in trouble without it, but I actually did better. I think it has to do with determined parents.

Neil (Mom and Dad's minister) came to see me next. He was a big help to Mom and Dad and gave them strength when they needed it most. He prayed a wonderful prayer for me and my family, and it really helped us.

It was then time for us to be a family, so Mom, Dad, and I set out for IU Hospital. Aunt Michelle somehow arranged to get us a suite at IU. They said it was not possible, but my Aunt Michelle is very determined. On the way, we stopped at the chapel so I could get baptized, not because I felt I had to but because the grandparents thought it was a good idea. So even though Mom and Dad knew I was sinless and would go to heaven, they baptized me out of love for my grandmas and grandpas. Neil prayed again, and there wasn't a dry cheek in the chapel.

Jane brought me my first toy, a beautiful teddy bear with a rattle. It was fun to play with it. We got to our room at IU, and it was perfect—nice and private and big. The first thing Mom did was nap, while Dad and I watched cartoons (I prefer *Looney Toons*).

We had lots of visitors tonight—all wonderful friends of Mom and Dad from church and work, and neighbors. Everyone made me feel so loved. It's nice to have so many new friends. Even more of them called and left notes. It's really great to be so popular.

Uncle Phil brought in his video camera to take some pictures, even though Dad didn't think it was a great idea. As it turned out, Dad cherishes this tape more than anything. I guess it goes to show that even the best dad is human.

Night of Day 2

Dad and I watched a basketball game tonight. It was an NBA finals game. Chicago won. Dad slept.

We were all lying in bed ready for sleep, and Dad was just about ready to call the nursery and have them get me. That's when Aunt Terri called Dad at 11:15 p.m. to see what was up. Dad told her he was going to put me in the nursery, and Aunt Terri said, "No way!" She said I needed to be held at all times by loving friends and family. Dad couldn't agree more, so he told the nurses just to keep checking on us, and they did so well. Aunt Terri arrived at 1:30 a.m. to relieve Dad because he was tired. She read me nursery rhymes and held and rocked me. I could tell she had lots of experience being a mom.

It was a good day.

Day 3 – June 5, 1991

It was a family day for me. I was spending the whole day with Mom and Dad at IU. Grandma and Grandpa came to visit me in the morning and brought Aunt Barbara along. I love seeing relatives. They held me for a long time. Grandma did the most holding. It was a fun morning.

Dad took me outside to see the world at 11:30 a.m. He felt I needed some fresh air, and he probably did, too. We walked over to Arby's to get Mom a shake—chocolate, of course. I got to see the sun (which my eyes didn't like at first, but they got used to it) and the bluest sky ever. We watched a guy cut grass and smelled that fresh smell. I saw trees, a bird, clouds, and a semi (which let me know what diesel fuel smells like). It was a perfect day to be alive. We delivered the shake to Mom, as requested.

Grandma and Grandpa came in the afternoon, and it was so good to see them again. They held me a long time. Grandma did most of the holding. It was a fun afternoon. We spent the night as a threesome, with Mom doing most of the holding and always trying to push a bottle in my mouth. I guess she didn't realize I can't power eat like her and Dad.

About 2:00 a.m., I wasn't doing too well. In fact, Mom and Dad didn't think I would make it much longer. They made a big tearful fuss and said all kinds of goodbyes, thinking I was going somewhere. Quite frankly, the only place I was going was into Dr. David's arms as he carried me out of the room and rocked me in a rocking chair for hours. Then, about 4:00 a.m., my friend Nurse Caryn called to check on me. When she heard I wasn't doing so well, she rushed in. She found me in Dr. David's arms and both of us sound asleep. It was time for relief, so she took care of me the rest of the day (it was a long day for her).

Mom and Dad fell asleep waiting for the news, but later when Dad called at 5:30 a.m., I could hear his relief, and Caryn brought me back to Mom and Dad's room.

It was a good day.

Day 4 – June 6, 1991

It was another beautiful day, as expected. Today was another family day—just Mom, Dad, and me. Dad got a wheelchair and pushed Mom and me outside. We went for a long walk, and I got to see Dad's driving firsthand (Wow!).

We went over to a park, and I got to see birds, bushes, a hill, picnic tables, park benches, sidewalks made of brick, and a statue, and experience all kinds of great smells. I could tell it was making Mom and Dad feel lots better, especially since I had my big blue eyes open the whole trip. People came by and said I was so cute. I thought handsome was more appropriate, but I'll settle for cute at 79 hours old.

On our way back, I saw a Ferrari get a parking ticket. Dad said the owner could afford it. It was a great day with Mom and Dad. They are special.

I needed some help tonight because I was not very comfortable, but Caryn and Donna took care of it right away. I spent the whole night sleeping in the bed between Mom and Dad. Dad was so happy and thankful that Caryn got him a bed. I think he actually slept.

It was a good day.

Day 5 – June 7, 1991

It was another beautiful day, a perfect day to go to heaven.

Dad got Mom going early, and the three of us went for another walk. Well, Dad walked. Mom and I rode in the wheelchair. We went back to the park, and I got to go on a swing with Dad and a merry-go-round with them both. We were having a great time, and my eyes were open wide the whole time.

About 9:00, we headed back to our room. Dad showed me how to run on the way back as he pushed the wheelchair at full speed. It was fun. By the time I got back to the room, I wasn't feeling too good, but I still had no pain. Mom worried about that all the time, but thanks to her, I never felt pain at all. Dad took me from Mom's arms, and I looked at her and said, "I love you." Dad carried me to Caryn's office to have her check me over.

At 9:55 a.m., I looked up and saw heaven. It was beautiful. I took one last look at Dad and one last thought of Mom—the best parents any kid could hope for. But my view of heaven was too intriguing, and when Jesus called my name and asked me to follow him, I felt it was my time to go.

I know I left some hurting hearts behind, but that's the way God planned it. Each of you who hurts does so because of your love for my Mom and Dad and their family. Each kind thing you did, each prayer, each special card, each flower, each warm thought from you took a small slice of pain from my family's heart and replaced it with love. That's why you hurt now, so be thankful for it because your kindness and love earned it. Soon, that pain will again transform to love and allow us all to carry on and help us all find the way that will ensure we all meet in heaven someday.

I love you, Mommy. I love you, Daddy. I love you, Grandmas and Grandpas. I love all of you friends that I met and those I didn't, because if you have read this, you have touched my family's lives. Thank you so much for that.

Love,
Jonathan

It was a good day.

We were so glad that we had the funeral for Jonathan. It was so encouraging and rewarding to celebrate our son. Many people came and shared what the funeral meant to them. I can see now the fingerprints of God in having the memorial. He wanted us to celebrate his creation of Jonathan, and we could see a glimpse of his purposes in Jonathan's short life. John and I found out later that some who were not interested in faith or Jesus made commitments to put him in the driver's seat of their own lives because of Jonathan and our experience. How grateful we were for saying yes to a funeral. Just think how incredible their lives are going to be now having Jesus to talk to; that gave me such refreshment. Who knew? Praise God!

Prior to Jonathan, I was a young woman who desperately wanted to have a child but was deprived because of a chemotherapy drug that was used to save my life. But God, who loved me so much, made the impossible possible and the unimaginable imaginable. In this miracle pregnancy, he brought to me the most outstanding, phenomenal, personal gift. Imagine standing on the tippy top of a mountain looking out at all creation's breathtaking green earth, your eyes relishing in the most beautiful hues, the colors no one ever gets to see except from above. You look down into the Grand Canyon's expansive bottom and savor the magnificent, rainbow-stained beauty. That's the gift—this inexpressible experience of carrying my son in my womb and seeing his beautiful face at birth. Simply unexplainable! Back to my very early prayer to God, what I prayed before we ever started the pregnancy process. "Dear Lord, I so want to get pregnant. Please, Lord, don't let my hopes be dashed (Ps. 119:116). I want to feel life, a baby growing in my belly. I want to experience every stage of his growth, like the books tell me, from when his arms develop, his fingers, toes, eyelids. I want to feel every moment. I want the entire process—all of it, Lord, please. To feel every movement of my child. Oh, what must it be like to get big and fat and have everyone ask me when my baby's due and what I'm having. I want to read all the books. Please, Lord, could you give me this?"

It sounds funny, but what I had really wanted was the feeling of pregnancy. I never prayed about a child specifically or thought about carrying a baby in my arms, only about a baby in my womb. I craved so desperately to be pregnant, and God gave me that. God knows me better than I know myself. He knows the very best for me—not the easy, but the very best. He's giving me my heart's desire as he said he would (Ps. 37:4).

And what a fabulously fun blessing for John and me as we prepared to be parents for the first time. Think about this: We got to witness a miracle pregnancy. We saw our son alive, if only for a few days. We got to feel the love of special, endearing, deep friends as they helped with Jonathan. We experienced God's personal care for us all the way to the end and beyond with Jonathan. We saw others come to experience God and Jonathan in their lives. The list is endless.

And now, dear friend, because God has shown me his love personally and because I've experienced his power and found out that he is in control, I can take heart knowing that this was the best plan for John, Jonathan, and me. Through all my disappointments, God has revealed appointments for me, treasures I could have only come to see through this difficulty. I'm learning gratefulness in the midst of every difficulty, and that gratefulness brings real, true exuberance to my soul.

> *Consider it pure joy, my brothers and sisters, whenever you face trials of many kinds, because you know that the testing of your faith produces perseverance. Let perseverance finish its work so that you may be mature and complete, not lacking anything.*
>
> —James 1:2–4

Pure joy are the words God uses. Suffering equals pure joy in God's eyes. We are always looking at the back of the tapestry—the gnarled, knotty mess—when on the other side is a beautiful, artistic masterpiece.

I am learning that trusting God is profitable; it brings lightness and freedom to our hearts and our wondering minds. I now know who's holding my hand, who's getting me triumphantly through. I like the idea of being complete, lacking nothing. That's what I want.

Now, if the Lord had told me in advance what I would be facing, I would have said, "No, thank you. Send someone else, Lord, please. Not me." That's what Moses said when God asked him to deliver his people. "But Moses said, 'Pardon your servant, Lord. Please send someone else'" (Exod. 4:13). Do you ever feel like that? Do you wish someone else could take your place for that thing you're dreading but have to do? But now that it's over, although I would not want to go through it again ever, I can say that it was worth it all because of what I have gained. "The kingdom of heaven is like treasure hidden in a field. When a man found it, he hid it again, and then in his joy went and sold all he had and bought that field" (Matt. 13:44). That is what experiencing God in these trials has been like for me. I'm learning that God, who lavishly loves me and gives me good things always, well, he's worth selling it all for.

John and I decided to have Jonathan buried in John's birth town in northern Wisconsin next to his grandparents. We flew our pastor up to Elkhart Lake and had a graveside service. John's mom and dad were thrilled that we chose to have him buried nearby, and they faithfully took care of their grandson's grave until they passed away. We are sure and certain that Jonathan is in heaven with God, enjoying a magnificent life.

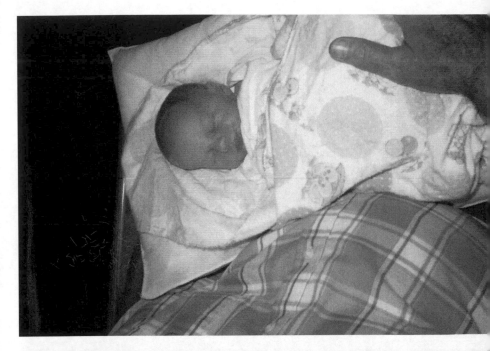
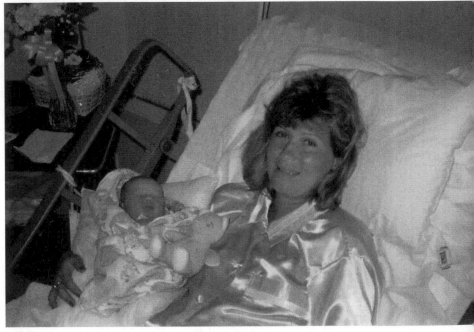

CHAPTER FIVE

God's Extravagant Gift

June 1991 was a blur. After my C-section and Jonathan's funeral, I longed to escape any duty-bound obligations. I wanted to cut and run, play hooky from my life, and make a getaway. But how could I skip out on my responsibilities? Who gets to do that? Life was still happening all around me. There were dinners to make, chores piling up, friends calling, and family checking in. Don't get me wrong; I was thankful for all of them, but I was burned out on living life—absolutely Krispy Kremed. I wanted to lie in bed for a week, cozied up with my favorite chocolate Oreos dipped in real whole milk, chocolate-covered cashews, and heavily buttered popcorn while binging on Hallmark movies, those sappy ones that end after the first kiss. I love knowing what's going to happen and that it's always something good.

It was a nice dream, but the reality was that if I did that, I would go completely berserk, and my mind would spin in a whirlwind. I had thoughts like what would we do with our life now? Baby? No baby? It had to be addressed; this was our future to think about. I don't have a personality that goes with the flow, does just what's in front of me, lives in the moment, and lets it all happen. No. No. I must have a plan, a super-controlled program. I'm type A, through and through. Logically, how could I even think about a baby again? Yet my mind kept sprinting to what's next.

Meanwhile, John was just happy to have no blueprint, no drama, no equation to solve, and no feelings to deal with. Chattering about weather conditions was the extent of our conversations. And even though I was exhausted, I just couldn't stop thinking about what was next for us.

When I wasn't thinking about the future, I thought of my sweet little Jonathan. With sharp aches penetrating my heart, I wondered if he had suffered. I wished I knew. No, I didn't want to know. He seemed so peaceful, so tranquil. I'd focus on that. But what must it have been like for him? Did he know that we loved him, that we cared for him and made sure, the best we could, that all his needs were met? Did he know? When our little Peaches would get a thorn in her paw, she'd come right to us so we could remove it. She knew we would take care of it for her. Did Jonathan know? God's the only one who knows that, and one day he can answer these things for me. But at the time, not knowing how Jonathan felt was my most difficult grief. It made my stomach hard and my body limp just pondering it. I wonder if this is how caregivers of dying loved ones feel. Caregivers spend so many hours consumed with how to relieve a loved one's pain, yet they don't always know how much pain their loved one is feeling, especially if the person can't speak. That is often the case at the end of life and with babies like Jonathan. It's a monumental burden for the caregiver who tries his or her prize-worthy best to relieve the suffering.

Oddly, when Jonathan passed, I had a great sense of relief. I knew he was no longer suffering. Watching him go through the dying process and not being able to help him was excruciating. So when he passed, I felt a peculiar sense of relief—and I felt ashamed because of it. I've subsequently spoken with others who've experienced the same relief. They say the same thing—we tend to feel guilty because we are so relieved. Apparently, it's quite normal. No more waiting for the inevitable to happen. Those sleepless nights and suffering days are finally over. It sounds so cold, so odd, but it's so true. It's real, and it's normal for the person who's on the front lines caring for their dying loved one.

John was raw. I could see it in his countenance, and I was feeling shredded up, too. Minutes felt like hours; hours felt like days of forced activity. The anchor to my soul, God, whom I have come to realize orchestrates all my circumstances, had thrown me a huge curveball, but I was learning to rely on him through it. First Thessalonians 5:18 says, "Give thanks in all circumstances; for this is God's will for you in Christ Jesus." God was going to have to put our shattered lives back together. If you were to ask me back then about having children, I would have said no thank you, not interested anymore.

But then came July. John was promoted, and we were moving to Michigan. Our life was blooming slowly like a new tender shoot standing tall in spring; our souls were beginning to thrive and flourish with new hope of a happy future.

"Honey, this could be just what the doctor ordered—or really what God has ordered," John said happily as we packed to move.

"It's a wonderful opportunity for your career, honey," I said, "and a chance for us to start fresh in a new area, a new state."

"I'm feeling really pumped about this opportunity," John said. "I feel motivated again. I'm actually living. Are we finally moving on from Jonathan's death?"

It seemed hard to believe, but I think we were. We picked a few cities near John's new Michigan office and spent a full day with our real estate agent looking for a place to live.

"What do you think about that cottage house on the lake?" I said. "I love the idea of waves and boats and fish and geese—well, maybe not geese on the front lawn. All that poop—yuck. You know, geese are mean. Europe uses them as guard dogs—uh, guard geese."

We laughed and talked through our options. "What's your favorite so far?" I asked. "I really like the newer home with the french doors to what would be your office on the first floor. Wish we knew who our friends were going to be, who the neighbors were. Wouldn't it be great if there was a neighborhood picnic we could go to and snoop to see who lives around us?"

John laughed. "Cindy, you're always 10 steps ahead. God will bring the friends and the perfect house."

"I know. You're right." I always appreciated his positive, truthful spin. Michigan is the land of a thousand lakes, so brilliantly we thought, let's live on a lake. The thing we forgot was that Michigan has two weeks of summer. Literally, everyone in the state goes up north at the same time. Why? Because it's the two weeks of summer. So maybe living on a frozen lake isn't that brilliant, but we pursued it anyway.

That evening, we returned to our hotel, totally exhausted from a packed day of looking for that perfect house. When we walked into our hotel room, ready to put our feet up, John noticed that someone had left us a message on our hotel phone. It was a frantic message from my friend Julie saying, "Cindy, there's an attorney trying to get a hold of you. It's good news!" Good news from an attorney? What in the world could it be?

Immediately we called the number.

The attorney answered in a deep, calm voice. "This is Steven. I'm an adoption attorney. Your name was given to me as a couple interested in adopting a child; and well, a baby has been born. We think you would be great parents for him." It was as sudden and pointed as that. Who, what, where, when, how—so many questions to ask. I wanted to shout my excitement all over this guy, whoever he was. Who was he, anyway? How did he get our number? I needed some composure—didn't want him thinking I was a lunatic. A baby had been born, and we could be his parents? Huh? Was this a joke? It was inconceivable. If his voice hadn't been so confident and measured, I would've felt spoofed.

Before our minds could discern what he was saying, his offer knocked us off our feet, and our emotions spoke. "We'd love to have him. Yes, yes, yes!" This was God's doing—no other possible explanation. We were sitting in the middle of Michigan when this attorney, from out of the sky, called our obscure, small-town hotel room to ask us if we wanted a baby. It was astonishing. How else on God's green earth could this have happened if God hadn't been involved? It wouldn't be until much later that the fire hose of questions flooding our minds would get answered, but we didn't care. A baby had been born for us. We were so excited we could hardly sleep that night.

"I feel so jittery inside," I said. "I think the excitement is overwhelming me and scaring me all at the same time. Don't you wonder what he looks like? Honey, is this the right thing?"

"We've waited so long, Cindy. This is 100 percent the right thing. This is from God who always has perfect plans for us."

"Yes, yes, yes. You are so right."

"Just like that, boom! We're going to be parents."

"I'll believe it when he's in my arms," I said. I'd come this close to motherhood before. "I wish this night was over and we were getting ready to pick him up right now."

"Me too."

"I have to get some supplies for our little guy. What should I dress him in? Remember that baseball outfit we got from Kerry for Jonathan? I'll bring that."

There was a rush of so much good coming into our lives—change we didn't ask for but that sought us out. This was so beyond what we could have ever hoped for.

We later found out how this all transpired. After we lost Jonathan, our wonderful ob-gyn made a call to a friend who worked as an adoption attorney to tell him our story and ask if there were any birth mothers considering adoption. Coincidentally, we had met this adoption attorney friend when we initially pursued adoption; he was the one who told us we would have to find a baby on our own. We had said no; the hill to adoption was too steep for us to scale. We felt it was impossible, unattainable, basically a needle in a haystack. My ob-gyn and I hadn't realized we had a mutual acquaintance; only God had known and ordained it, putting those impossible circumstances together.

We learned that the private adoption process required potential adoptive parents to write letters to the birth mother as a way for her to screen candidates. The decision was completely hers to make. The attorney would then take letters from a few possible adoptive parents and present them to the birth mother. How kind and thoughtful for the potential birth mom who must have been as overwhelmed as we were with the entire process. Imagine a grandma coming from a Chinese province to buy butter at Kroger. The many shelves are lined with butter, canola oil, plant butter, Amish butter, Irish butter, no-salt butter—so many butters. It would be overwhelming. She might end up leaving the store with no butter because she just can't decide. Imagine looking for parents for your child you have just given birth to. So we wrote our letter. Beginning it was an incredibly daunting task that might determine the biggest decision of our life—the decision we've been begging God to give us. Each word mattered. Each word needed God's touch. How in the world could we ever begin to understand what would mean the most to her?

As we sat down and thought about it, we realized that what we really wanted the birth mom to know was how much we would love, care for, and encourage her son. We wanted her to know that we would give him every opportunity for a tremendous life, that his possibilities would be endless and that he would never lack anything as much as we could give him. We wanted to console her and let her know that God had the best plan for her child and that we couldn't even imagine how hard this decision would be for her. Somehow we wanted to convey to her that it would be okay because God was taking ultimate care of her son who was precious in his eyes. If we'd learned anything, it was that. After too many rewrites to count, we received this promise from God through reading his Word: "This poor man called, and the LORD heard him; he saved him out of all his troubles. The angel of the Lord encamps around those who fear him, and he delivers them (Ps. 34:6–7).

The attorney brought the letters to the birth mom. We were very nervous. Had we said the right thing, the perfect thing, the thing that would make her choose us? We tried very hard to put ourselves in her shoes and sympathize with what she must have been going through. As we looked at life from her perspective, we felt burdened for her. Can you imagine making a decision about your child based on a letter? All we could do—the best and truest thing we could do—was put God in the center of what was happening. He gave us confidence that whatever the mother decided was the right decision for that little boy. The situation was so beyond our abilities or comprehension, yet we could see God revealing to us that there are no coincidences. So here we were—yet again—on another roller-coaster ride with God at the controls.

After reading all the letters, the mother decided on us. We would be her son's parents. Throwing my fists in the air, I yelled at the top of my lungs, "We won!" It was as if we'd won the lottery. We did win our lottery. We were so thrilled. *Thank you, God!* We couldn't wait to get back home from Michigan. We forgot all about buying a home and jumped on the next plane back to Indianapolis to tell all our friends the fantastic news. Our poor friends had ridden the roller coaster with us from the very beginning, from the chug-chug-chug up the steep inclines to the race down in pure ecstasy—from grief in Jonathan's death to now the enthusiasm of our son's arrival. Imagine being our friends.

A party was going on in our home when we got there. Everyone had pitched in to get all the immediate supplies we would need for our son's arrival. A beautiful, contemporary, white crib arrived with a giraffe bumper pad and quilt to match. There were bottles, the cutest boy clothes ever, and little jean bib overalls that later became my favorite to dress him in. All the essentials were suddenly filling our home. What a treasure of superb friends. Everyone was involved in this great blessing the Lord was giving us.

The astonishing call from that adoption attorney on the evening of July 5 at our hotel in Lansing, Michigan, just happened to come on my birthday. Think about it. This unfathomable gift of our boy was given to me by God on my birthday. I just can't believe it. It was the best birthday gift I will ever receive in my entire life, hands down. Only God could give me a treasure like this.

John wanted to name our son Sam—you know, like Uncle Sam since he was born on the Fourth of July—but I just couldn't do it. We picked Adam because it's the name God chose for the very first man. We figured God must love that name to have chosen it for the first man he created. I later learned that the name Adam actually means red dirt. Get this! Adam's a redhead. I had no idea. Another fingerprint of God.

Before we knew it, the day came, and we boarded our attorney's private jet to pick up Adam. We felt like we were in the TV show *The Amazing Race*, bouncing from house hunting in Michigan to picking up our son in Indiana. What a whirlwind, with God at the helm. Every intricate detail was being worked out. From Jonathan's going to heaven, to an ob-gyn who God burdened to help us find a child we didn't ask for, to an attorney we already knew, to a birth mom who said yes to our letter, to dear friends who helped get us ready for our baby—so many details had come together for Adam, John, me, and even Jonathan. Once more, John and I were reminded of Proverbs 16:9: "In their hearts humans plan their course, but the LORD establishes their steps." I often hear that everything happens for a reason. Yes, it does—God's reason. God guides hearts wherever he pleases (Prov. 21:1).

After the flight in our attorney's private jet to a small Indiana town, we went to the local hospital and then to the nursery. John and I were put in a small room, and a young, slender nurse came in and introduced herself. She said her name was Kimmy, our son's nurse. Wow! She knows Adam already. There was so much I wanted to ask her, but not a word came to mind. She inserted a video in the 1980s-looking TV about how to give a baby a bath and then went to get Adam. The 10' x 8' room had an old-fashioned oak rocking chair with a quilted pad on it and an oak dresser with a TV on top playing our baby-washing video. Three sides of the room had windows, hardly a private meeting to be introduced to your son for the first time. The room smelled like Johnson & Johnson baby shampoo. The hanging fluorescent lights lit every nook and cranny and brightened the white linoleum floor. The pattern was completely worn off but still looked hospital clean. My mind wandered to the birth mom. Was she still there? Was anyone with her?

"Honey," I said to John, "this is so surreal. A video on giving a baby a bath? Really?"

"Maybe it's a real problem. Maybe babies get injured by parents giving them a bath. Who knows?"

John always had a reason for everything. Whatever the reason, I was too excited to watch. It was all so unthinkable. Here we were waiting for our child—hear that, our child—in this tiny room. It sounded crazy. My mind was everywhere, my heart thumping out of my chest. *Lord God, please calm us.* I wonder what he looks like. I'm sure he's perfect. God picked him for us. I hope he's okay with that tiny, loud prop jet we're traveling in. Our attorney told us that newborns love jets, that they're a pacifying lullaby for them. "He'll be fine," John said. "It's all going to be great."

Then the door opened, and in an instant, we went from a childless couple to parents. We were Mom and Dad. There he was, our little pumpkin, as we affectionately called him because of his beautiful head of red hair. Adam was beautiful, more perfect than I'd imagined, definitely designed by God for us personally. Who could do a better job than God himself? Adam weighed 7 pounds 8 ounces and was long and slender. He looked at us as though to say, "Who are you?" He had the most gorgeous, sparkling blue eyes

I'd ever seen—just like John's. They had something in common already. All we could think was *Wow! What is happening here? We're this boy's parents! We are parents at this very moment. Finally!*

We carefully picked him up from his bassinet so we could hold him. As brand-new parents, we were initially tentative like we could break him or something, but that lasted only a second before we were squeezing, hugging, and coddling him as crazy parents in love do. He was so soft and smelled so sweet, just like babies smell when they're all cleaned up. Maybe the nurses had given him a bath in Johnson & Johnson baby shampoo. Boy, those nurses were sticklers for bathing, and hence our video. Adam was very calm and peaceful as if he were taking it all in. I was so thankful because if he had started to cry, I would have felt that he didn't want us, that he didn't like us. I was feeling slightly insecure.

It was a day for the history books of our little family, a monumental day with so many undiscovered feelings—excitement, fear, joy, a little sadness. All those years of waiting and charting and searching for a baby, and then our short time with Jonathan—all led to this moment. I've realized that God is not bound by my time frame. I can pray, and at the same time the thing I've prayed for could already have happened because God is not bound by my linear timeline. In this case, years of what seemed like unanswered prayer for a baby and so much heartbreak had led to this day, to our son in God's way and in his time, not mine.

Adam slept through the entire flight home just as our attorney said he would. All my worrying was for nothing. When our plane touched down, wheels screeching to a halt, I thought for sure that Adam would start screaming, and then what would I do? But no. He slept right through the shrieking halt. We were met with a huge crowd of well-wishers, like a ticker tape parade. What exceptional friends! It humbled me that they all came to meet our son. And with that, our new life with our new little boy began.

Years ago, I came across Isaiah 55:8–11, and still today, it anchors me to this unexpected, unpredictable whirlwind of a life I have. I'll sum it up in my own words: my ways and thoughts are not yours, declares the Lord; they are higher, heavenly, and better, and they accomplish all my plans.

Today, the Monday morning quarterback view is quite clear. God's fingerprints of love are all over the story of how we received our hearts' desire. The events leading up to having a child didn't happen as we would have logically planned—young couple marries, gets pregnant, has a healthy boy, and lives happily ever after. But I'm so thankful they didn't because God's plan so far exceeded ours. We still often share this with Adam.

All my family's days were already written in God's book before one moment began: "Your eyes saw my unformed body, all the days ordained for me were written in your book before one of them came to be" (Ps. 139:16). This plan includes the day of Jonathan's heavenly homecoming. It was the Father's plan, and I had to submit to it. This same plan brought us Adam, and God has knit our hearts together by making the three of us a family. That's what God does for his children. He doesn't promise easy. He promises good. "Do not be afraid, little flock, for your Father has been pleased to give you the kingdom" (Luke 12:32).

Reading in my Bible about Moses's birth, I see God's goodness in the difficult circumstances surrounding his tumultuous life (Exod. 1:1–2, 2:1–10). Moses's mother was a Hebrew when the Hebrew people were enslaved by the Egyptians. When she was pregnant, the Egyptian Pharaoh ordered all Hebrew boys to be killed at birth. When Moses was born, his mom hid him. After three months, though, she could no longer hide him, so she made a waterproof basket, put him in it, and placed it on the Nile River. Can you imagine being that mom and having to abandon your child in a river with the hopes that someone would find him before he drowned?

By God's design, Pharaoh's daughter found Moses crying in the basket and felt sorry for him. She asked her attendants to find the mother, have her breastfeed him until he was weaned, and then bring him back for her to raise. When Moses was weaned, his mom brought him to Pharaoh's daughter, and he became her son.

This sounds so tragic. But having feared so long for her son's life, Moses's mother surely found relief knowing he was safe. His adoption by Pharaoh's daughter was a blessing in the midst of terrible circumstances, but it was just the beginning of God's huge plan for Moses. Before Moses was even born, God had a plan for him to lead the Hebrews, likely including his dear mother, away from the harsh Pharaoh and into Canaan, the land of milk and honey.

> The LORD said, "I have indeed seen the misery of my people in Egypt. I have heard them crying out because of their slave drivers, and I am concerned about their suffering. So I have come down to rescue them from the hand of the Egyptians and to bring them up out of that land into a good and spacious land, a land flowing with milk and honey."
> —Exod. 3:7–8

Oh, what plans the Lord has for us, his people!

Adam's birth mom, for whatever reason, could not raise her son, so with the help of attorneys and letters, she decided to give him to us. This story had been written in God's book before the foundations of the world. Imagine that! We talked about a birth mom making decisions and attorneys helping the process, letters being written; meanwhile, God had the course of action completely done, finished, in his book. It's amazing to think about that, isn't it? I can't see tomorrow, but God sees it, and he's the architect, the designer, the builder, and the decorator. Sounds a little similar to Moses, doesn't it?

I'm often asked how the experiences of birthing a child and adopting one compare. Do I have special affection for one more than the other?

The answer is a hard no. There is absolutely no difference in my mind between birthing your child and adopting him. I've found that love grows in your heart as you give yourself to your child. Open your heart wide, and let God fill you with that momma-baby love connection whether he or she is of your flesh or not. God does it. He knits our hearts together, and it's extraordinarily perfect and beautiful. So press in, do not be discouraged or unbelieving in the promise; he will knit you together.

When Adam was growing up, I would tell him about his brother Jonathan in heaven. I would also tell him the story of how God brought him to us. I would tell him how God had him birthed by his birth mom and then given to us to raise because it was the very best plan for him and me and Dad and his birth mom—everyone involved. I would read Psalm 139 to him often, about how he had been knit by God in his mother's womb and how God had plans too wonderful for him to know and how God knows us before we know ourselves. I told him that if he fled from God's presence, God would still be there guiding him with his powerful right hand, holding and protecting him (Ps. 139:7–8, 10). I told Adam that God had made him wonderful and perfect, just how he'd planned him to be, and that all his days had been written down before one of them came to be (Ps. 139:16). Dear reader, let us all take comfort in that truth.

Of course, I can't choose between my boys, but I would not change God's plan one bit. If Jonathan hadn't passed away and been taken into our Father's loving arms, I would not have Adam today. All this was so very hard, but it was so good at the same time. God "turned my wailing into dancing" (Ps. 30:11).

Adam is now 27 and lives on the West Coast. He loves climbing mountains, traveling the world, and helping others. His career is in the health-care industry—no shock considering how deeply he cares for people. If I may brag as a mom who loves her boy, he's compassionate and loving, and he has quite a dynamic personality. He's handsome with a head of beautiful, thick, red hair, and he is well-liked by everyone who meets him.

Adam was born with a bout of colic. If you're a parent of a colicky child, you know how exhausting and frustrating it can be. The doctors and resource materials all say they will grow out of it. Parents are to make sure all their needs are met and then let them cry it out. Well, let me tell you, if you're a mom, the last thing in the world you want to do is let your child cry, cry, cry that piercing wailing. I put our vacuum cleaner next to his crib and turned it on, and Adam would fall right to sleep. There are crazy remedies for colic, like strapping you child in a car seat or pumpkin seat, placing him on the clothes dryer, and turning it on. Adam loved it. As my dad would say, somehow we muddle through (I believe it's a saying by Henry Ford).

Adam's adolescent and teen years were pleasurable for us as parents because he had a lighthearted zest for life, and there was never drama around him. He had a healthy respect for authority. Many parents experience a lot of grief with their children and feel relief when they leave home. I remember friends telling me they were so happy their children were going off to college because life with them in the home had been so hard. I feel for them, but this was not our experience with Adam. When he left for college, I mourned as if he had died. For three days, nothing could console me. Nothing! It was a horrible pain. It wasn't just that he was going to college; it was what the whole season of life meant. He was becoming a man, never to be a child again. I was not prepared for that. The saving grace was that on the third day, I woke up, and the feeling was completely gone. God must have relieved me, because I was set free from that piercing sorrow. "Rejoicing comes in the morning" (Ps. 30:5). Our kids are supposed to leave the nest and become all God wants them to be. We are supposed to push them out of the nest and let them fly. I came to accept that Adam had to leave to become a pillar in society. I told Adam from birth that he was the *greatest* gift God could ever have given me for my birthday, that there would never be a gift more desirable than he was. I would often tell God that, too.

Is that true, though? It seemed so to me. When Adam was about 10, we made a trip to Gasparilla Island, Florida, for vacation. It was once again my birthday, the anniversary of when we first learned about Adam, and I was taking a walk along the spectacular shoreline, the sun high in the sky, not a cloud anywhere. The ocean was so tropically blue and glistening. The homes on the sandy shoreline had a coastal architecture, each painted a soft pastel color. Each house had the most unusual, colorful, full, blooming plants that I felt like I was in a fairyland. As I strolled, I reflected on the precious son God had given me. I talked with the Lord, thanking him for his great gift. *Lord, you could never give me a present more precious than Adam.*

I neared the end of my walk, heading for the long, stately pier in front of our condo. The water was crystal clear that day. I could see the pristine, sandy bottom much like the Caribbean. I was admiring it when right in front of me a huge manatee popped his head out of the water and looked right into my eyes. He was so close I could have touched his nose. He came out of nowhere. You must understand something. I *love* manatees and had never seen one in my 20 years of going to Florida beaches. The Lord spoke to me at that moment, much like when Jonathan had passed. "Cindy," God said to me, "I have been giving you good gifts all your life. I have many, many more good gifts ahead for you." I can't imagine what God could possibly do to surpass his gift of Adam to me. I can't comprehend anything greater. But he wants to give me more and more of his inexhaustible treasures, and he wants to do that for you, too.

When God puts our lives together as only he can, it's a profoundly incredible, white-knuckle adventure—white-knuckle because we can't see or understand his future plan. We have to take our hands off the steering wheel and let him do his job, or we could end up in the ditch, devastated from trying to make it all happen in our straightforward pathway. It is God who orchestrates and directs and puts into place all these events for his good purpose.

CHAPTER SIX

What? Again?

Nothing happens to me or you without God's involvement. His words and my experience have taught me that he's orchestrating even the worst situations for his good result.

As I write to you in the wee hours of the morning, outside my kitchen window overlooking our dark, black lake is the most spectacular moon I've ever seen. It's called, I'm told by Laura, my neighbor and friend across the lake, a harvest moon. Vivid orange and *gigantic*, it's covering a fourth of the sky. It's spectacular, beautiful, and completely mesmerizing. (Laura and I will often text in the wee hours. She's the only one up. It's a special bond we have together.) I'd like to brag to you a little by telling you that I know the artist. He designed that moon, the sun, the stars, the whole darned thing. The Bible says he brings the sun out of a tent in heaven each day. He's designing our stories, too—yours and mine.

I'm waiting by faith for God to give me what's best for my next steps. *Cindy, keep focused,* I remind myself. *Don't get lost now. You've come too far. You do believe. Lord, help me believe you now. Help me, God, because I do know the truth, that precious eternity truth that you have the best next outcome.*

Here is the prayer of my heart:

> *I lift up my eyes to the mountains—*
>   *where does my help come from?*
> *My help comes from the LORD,*
>   *the Maker of heaven and earth.*
> *He will not let your foot slip—*
>   *he who watches over you will not slumber;*
> *indeed, he who watches over Israel*
>   *will neither slumber nor sleep.*
>
> —Ps. 121:1–4

God never sleeps. He's watching over me and will not let me slip. I'm waiting for that supernatural peace that transcends all human understanding to come and guard my heart and my mind. God's peace, when it comes, is magnificent. It envelopes my whole body and infiltrates every throbbing crevice of my jittery mind. All those raw nerve ends are soothed with his ointment. Nothing less than that will do. Philippians 4:7 says, "And the peace of God, which transcends all understanding [that's his soothing ointment], will guard your hearts and your minds in Christ Jesus." That's what my grandma had, that kind of confidence. So did the Virgin Mary when an angel came to her to tell her she was carrying Jesus, the Son of God, in her womb. After hearing this news, she replied, "I am the Lord's servant. . . . May your word to me be fulfilled" (Luke 1:38). That's faith with no evidence against all odds. If I could only have that faith.

In the daylight, I could see the leaves in full color—bright yellow, glowing oranges, and deep scarlets. I was driving up a steep hill one day when my eyes glanced into the sky ahead, and for the first time that season, I caught the beauty of the trees, fascinated by the artistry of those vivid colors. I longed to pull over and have a moment to relish the picture-perfect scene—a Monet painting coming to life on an exquisite day. *Thank you, Lord.*

Adam was finishing his senior year of high school. Books were nonexistent now. The class parties and practical jokes were the graduates' constant airstream. *Why am I so tentative about his going to college?* He was already so responsible and making great decisions. John and I were proud of the man he'd become. I just needed to throw off those senseless, rogue, defective feelings. I'm going to miss him so much. He's such a presence in our home. We lived for him and his schedule. Every day revolved around Adam. John may have struggled even more than I because he and Adam were best buds, pals. They did everything together. John even helped coach his lacrosse team. Practice, practice, practice with constant hard balls thrown around our house and at the beach. Every possible sliver of land was fair game for lacrosse practice. We loved having him home. For 16 years, he had been our central focus. That's what we parents do.

Rather than dwelling on all my disparaging worries of missing Adam, I began praying that we would have a great last summer together before he left for college. I decided to think about all the adventures we could have together—shopping for the perfect cotton shorts or the latest leather sandals with not too thick of a sole, which is always an adventure. We could eat lunches at The Cheesecake Factory or Yats, one of Adam's favorites; maybe boating in Nashotah or bike at Sanibel Island. I have to admit I was a little concerned I wouldn't see much of him when summer hit; after all, he was a senior sports fanatic and a social dude, always on the go with his buds. It should be that way, I knew. I had to let this go so I could enjoy this most treasured time of mothering. I hoped it would be mothering in a positive way and not as Adam saw it: "Mom, stop *momming* me!" *Lord, please give us precious mom-and-son time together*, I prayed. There was a lot to do before school let out, not to mention the start of the graduation party competition. Why did it always have to be a competition? Why did everyone try to outdo one another at their graduation open houses? Who had the best food, the best entertainment, the best decorations? Ugh! Where to even begin? I felt so pressured to make it over the top for him. I had to get on top of the rivalry challenge, though.

I had life-sized, free-standing posters of Adam made and positioned them around the house. They were always spooking me since they looked so real. We also had a root beer float station—a big hit. Of course, I made my delicious, flavorful Rachael Ray burgers, a favorite of Adam's friends.

The next week was my annual mammogram appointment. They were always completely uneventful, like going to the grocery store for milk. *At least I'm on time*, I thought, looking at the large wall clock behind the sign-in sheet. *Why are there always so many women at this breast imaging center? Not even an empty chair.* I was feeling conspicuous standing there, and I wondered what others were thinking as I scoped out the crowded room. Statistically, every sixth person in that room would be or had been diagnosed with breast cancer. How depressing! *Cindy, go to your happy place*, as Adam would say. *Remember, you're at the grocery store for milk.* I was called to the back area by a young, smiley nurse who improved my get-this-over-with experience with her pleasantries. For a minute, I forgot about the standing room only and the waiting room stare-down. We chit-chatted on our way to the mammography area; then I had the mammogram and went home. Simple, as I had assumed, and expectedly uneventful.

Two days later, I noticed a voicemail from the breast care center. The message said they needed my correct address. I told myself, *This happens. Doctors' offices don't always have the correct information. This happens—not often, but it does happen.* When I called to give the address, the nurse said she wanted me to come in for further evaluation. This, she said, was quite normal and generally nothing. Sneaky, but her calmness and lack of concern made my revved-up heart calm down. She was very believable, so I thought nothing of it.

I went back to the center the next morning, this time with John. From very early on in our marriage, after all my health issues, John insisted on being at all of my appointments. He's very interested in firsthand information when it comes to my health, an attribute for which I am very grateful. He's very caring. I feel confident when he's in my corner. I call it my umbrella from the storms. He knows I'm more serene when he's there. But with him taking time away from work to come to this appointment, I had an unsettling feeling that this was becoming more than just a milk run. My nerves were growing to epic proportions. I couldn't turn off the disparaging voice in my head.

"Honey, can you hold me and remind me this is nothing?"

John held me and dissuaded my wayward thoughts. He was always so good at bringing right perspectives intertwined with hope.

God's Word says to take every thought captive and make it obedient to God. So I knew I shouldn't let my mind conjure up worrisome thoughts. Instead, I should think things that are true and lovely and excellent and praiseworthy (1 Thess. 5:18, Phil. 4:8). As far as keeping my ducks in a row and ordering my thoughts, well, I didn't even know where my ducks were. I was far from holding my thought of breast cancer captive and having positive, lovely, and true thoughts. Instead of taking it captive, I stayed in a very dark place, remembering the three friends I'd just buried in the last three years—all from breast cancer and all younger than I was. I was there while they were dying, in the thick odor-filled places where moaning and emotions touched the sky. Sadness and grief pamphlets littered the rooms. No fairness, liveliness, or energy—only the substantial dark gloom of an end. Looking back, I'm stunned at how I was able to console and give hope. It had to be all God. There were so many grievous memories. Young moms should not ever die. Altogether, I'd been at six friends' dying bedsides. This was not a little thing to me, and the vivid memories still haunt me.

The nurse called my name for the second time. I wished I could just walk out the exit door as if this thing was not happening.

"Sir, you cannot come back here," the nurse said. "I will call you back when she's finished."

"Honey, I'll be fine," I said.

As John turned back to the waiting room, I caught his facial expression. He was quite annoyed. John was the master at getting into hospital rooms, physicians' offices, radiology rooms, you name it, so to not be beside me for this was difficult for him. Interestingly, though, when John went back to sit, he noticed a friend from church in the waiting room.

"Mary, how are you?" he asked.

"Good, John. Is Cindy here?"

"Yes. There have been some complications."

"I'm so sorry to hear that. Did you know I had breast cancer 10 years ago?"

"Oh, Mary, I didn't know. It looks like you're doing great now. Is everything okay?"

"Yes, I'm doing wonderful."

Thankfully, Mary stayed to talk with John, and I know this was a tremendous comfort to him. Their encounter was no coincidence; it was definitely God in action, designed to help my struggling husband through a difficult wait for unknown news. First Thessalonians 5:18 reminds us that we are to give thanks in all circumstances, for such is God's will. This moment was already designed and written in God's book before the world was made. In Psalm 139:16, David wrote, "All the days ordained for me were written in your book before one of them came to be." Just to see her 10 years out from her breast cancer was a real glimmer of hope for us both. I'm always amazed at how God brings comfort at just the right time through just the right people. God was using Mary to give us a big, warm, enveloping hug of trust, for he is the God of comfort. Second Corinthians 1:4 says God "comforts us in all our troubles, so that we can comfort those in any trouble with the comfort we ourselves receive from God."

The radiologist called us both into his office. *This is not a good thing*, I thought. There were two large monitors on his desk, and I figured those were my breast images on the screen. There was no chit-chat, just right to the point. "Cindy, you have spots on both breasts. I can't be sure if they're just calcification or more serious breast cancer."

Cancer. Really, cancer? Unbelievable! How, God, could you bring this into my life again? This was just a grocery store run. He was my trustworthy, loving Father by this time. Why would he make me go through this again? I could not understand. *I've been here before*, I reminded myself, trying to bring composure against my erratic, unmanageable thoughts. But this news hit like a tsunami. All I could think was that I'm going to suffer and die.

The next day, I went to the breast care center for a biopsy. I felt so sorry for my poor self—as if I were the only one in the world going through this process. In my mind I was, though the breast care center waiting room was packed with women dealing with breast cancer and anomalies just like I was. What a dangerous place. My mind was consumed. I call it the "devil's war room" because it's the place where I heard lies such as God is not good and he doesn't actually have my best interest at heart. It's not exactly surprising since the devil himself is called the father of all lies (John 8:44). Looking back, I'm reminded of something C. S. Lewis wrote:

> The smallest good act today is the capture of a strategic point from which, a few months later, you may be able to go on to victories you never dreamed of. An apparently trivial indulgence in lust or anger today is the loss of a ridge or railway line or bridgehead from which the enemy may launch an attack otherwise impossible.[7]

Make no mistake; today's battle does matter. It was not a time for self-pity and indulgences. I could see the setup of the enemy taking

---

7. C.S. Lewis, *Mere Christianity* (New York: Macmillan Publishing Company, 1952), 117.

territory to attack me. What I needed was hopeful belief that would get me to strategic victories. I had already learned all this through my previous cancer, but somehow I was still in a bad way.

A nurse came to the waiting room and called my name. I was tired of waiting-room nerves dominating my body, ruling my thoughts and skin and heart. *Here we go.* The imaging room was dimly lit. The first step was to insert a very long piece of wire into each breast at the point of the nodule. There were four nurses and a technician doing this, and they had a lot of trouble locating the nodules and inserting the wires. It was so tense for everyone. *God, please, please help them get this done. It's so awkward and uncomfortable.* I felt for the technician who clearly had done this procedure many times, yet you'd think it was her first maneuver—same as those poor nurses who could never find my veins to draw blood. What a nightmare!

God had workers everywhere in this difficult process. I learned later that two of the four nurses in that room were praying for me— nurses whom I'd never met before yet selflessly cared about me. As we were leaving the office, John and I ran into a woman from our church who would not stop talking. I was beside myself, having been through hell with those wires sticking out of my breasts. I just wanted her to go away and stop talking. I was the opposite of the two kind women in the sonogram room who prayed for me. Sometimes it's nearly impossible for me to be loving, especially when I've just had wires hanging out of my breasts.

After a short drive to the hospital for the surgical biopsy, we headed home. The car ride was eerily quiet; neither of us said a word. The doctor would call me the next day when the results came in. What a wait that was. We waited all day, and finally at 7:30 p.m., she called.

"I have terrible news. You have breast cancer in both breasts," she said, just like that. Only one question came to my mind. "Am I going to die?" I asked her. After all, this was not my first cancer; and what about my friends who had died of breast cancer?

The doctor said she didn't think so but wanted me to come into the office in the morning to go over the options. *Great! She didn't think I was going to die!* I hung up the phone, turned to Adam who was waiting in the living room, and burst into tears. He held me in his now big, strong arms. He had become such a well-rounded, compassionate adult. What comfort my son was to me in that moment! John sped into the driveway from work, and we all huddled together in tears. It was good to cry our eyes dry. What a release of boiling, painful sadness!

That night, I couldn't sleep. I was as awake as though it were noontime. My mind just wouldn't stop worrying that cancer was all over my body. It kept reminding me of my deceased friends and all the physical pain they'd endured. What about their husbands and children? John sensed my turmoil, held me in his arms, and prayed for me. As he held me, I could feel God giving me supernatural peace. It had to be God because nothing natural could have provided this kind of comfort, a feeling that it would all be okay and I was going to be fine—so unlike me, so brand-new. *Oh, God, can I stay in this feeling forever, please?* I had never felt God's peace in such a clear way. My body went from tense to calm, like a soft, warm blanket swaddling me. It was so unnatural. Before I knew it, the alarm went off. Wow! I'd slept through to the alarm. After being so wound up in the night, you'd think I was running a marathon. It was time to get up and go to the doctor's appointment.

I took a few minutes to call Elizabeth my internist and fill her in. She was a close, personal friend and fellow Christian. Her response astounded me: "Cindy, you are highly favored by God because he trusts you with this big thing. You're special."

I'm sure special all right! Her words reminded me of Mary's story in the Bible when the angel of the Lord said she was highly favored and would be the mother of Jesus. Mary thought that was a strange introduction. Well, same with me.

Dr. Cook was actually on time. I guess when you're diagnosed with cancer, you get preferential treatment because I don't think I'd ever had a prompt breast appointment before. John and I were ushered into a small room with dim lights, a round cherry-wood dining table with dark firm seats, and mauve wallpaper—interesting ambiance for being told you have cancer, almost like a spa room. My female breast surgeon was in her mid-40s, tall and thin. She seemed compassionate and capable. We sat together around the table as she explained what stage cancer each breast was in and how my only options were total mastectomies. The previous radiation from my Hodgkin's disease had made all my breast tissue bad, causing my breast cancer. The very thing that had saved my life was now possibly going to kill me if I didn't cut my breasts off and get rid of the bad tissue. How unfortunate is that? The good news was that I had no decisions to make such as whether to have a lumpectomy (removal of the mass only) or a complete mastectomy (removal of the entire breast). Since all the tissue was bad, it all had to go.

Early in the morning before leaving for this appointment, I had opened my favorite devotional, *Morning and Evening* by Charles Spurgeon. Sometimes, you need to hear from another person's encouragement rather than foraging for your own. This day's reading said, "My Heavenly Father knows what he's doing."[8] Wow! How I needed to know that this sickness would not end in death, that the Lord determines how far the waves of pain can go. "This far you may come and no farther" (Job 38:11). Spurgeon went on to say:

> [God's] fixed purpose is not the destruction, but the instruction of His people. . . . The God of providence has limited the time, manner, intensity, repetition, and effects of all our sicknesses; each throb is decreed, each

---

8. Charles H. Spurgeon, *Morning and Evening*, Google Books.

sleepless hour predestined, each relapse ordained. . . .
Nothing great or small escapes the ordaining hand of
Him Who numbers the hairs of our head.[9]

God knew what he was doing in bringing this cancer down my
path. It would not end in death. The pain would not destroy me but
instruct, teach, refine, build up, strengthen, and bring resolve to me
so that when it was over, I would be a mighty warrior of hope to
myself and those around me. What well-being I received from those
absolutely true, life-filling words. I determined to share Spurgeon's
words with my breast surgeon. After all she must hear in a day—such
hopelessness, sadness—I wanted her to know that it was not all on
her back. It was God's deal, not hers. So before I left that morning, I
made a copy, folded it, and took it to Dr. Cook.

At the appointment, she explained the procedure to us. I would
come in at 7:00 a.m. to be prepared for surgery at 10:00 a.m. She
would remove my nipple, cut a long incision across my breast, and
remove all the tissue, cancerous and noncancerous. It all had to
go, along with either a single lymph node or all of them around
my breast, depending on how far the cancer had spread. *God, this
information is a little much, don't you think? Thank you for reminding me
in Ephesians 1:11 that this moment has been predestined according to your
plan and that you're working out everything according to your will. This
is your plan, your purpose, your will. I'm so glad I took moments with you
so I could know who you are in all this—because what I really want to do
is totally freak out.*

Then Dr. Cook explained that she would do the same with
the other breast. When she finished, which she believed would
be about three hours later, the plastic surgeon would come in and

---

9. Charles H. Spurgeon, "Evening," August 17, 2011, *Devotionals by C. H.
Spurgeon, Christian Forums*, https://www.christianforums.com/threads/
devotionals-by-c-h-spurgeon.7515074/page-8#post-58317260.

place something like deflated balloons in each breast. This was the reconstruction part of the surgery, which would take another three hours. When the stitches across each breast were removed 10 days later, my plastic surgeon would begin injecting sterile water into the implanted balloons and slowly inflate them over a six-month period, stretching the skin to make room for the implants.

This felt like too much to me. "Dr. Cook, I'm not sure I'm interested in reconstruction. Let's just get the cancer out and call it a day."

"Cindy, you're a young woman. I think you will be disappointed if you don't have breasts. Imagine when you go to the beach or to a formal event."

"Maybe you're right," I said reluctantly. "I hadn't thought about any of that. Sounds like you think it's best and I should do it?"

"I absolutely do."

Poor John was sitting in the background, absorbing all the information thrown at us in that darkened room. I'm sure he was just happy to hear I was going to most likely live. It was very surreal to think about breast image at this point. Today, I'm glad she pressed me.

When she finished her synopsis, it was my turn to talk. I really had nothing to say about the procedure except *let's go*; but what I did want to discuss was my copy of Spurgeon's devotional from that morning. I explained that I was a woman of faith, and my devotional that day said that God is the organizer of our days. He's the planner, the caretaker of persons. He brings the perfect doctor for the patient. This cancer was in his hands, too. I wanted her to know how grateful I was that he brought me to her to fix me up. I gave her the copy, and she was very moved. I could tell her demeanor of professionalism had turned to relief. I know God was speaking to her, too.

Later that week, we learned my surgery was scheduled for six weeks later. I blew a gasket. Six weeks was way too long for a woman with breast cancer. I tried to get it changed, but there was no way. "Impossible," I was told. The problem was finding availability to coordinate two specific doctors along with their staff for surgery and reserving an operating room all at the same time. *I knew I shouldn't have done the reconstruction. Then I could get in sooner. Don't they know I have cancer? Schedules are keeping me from lifesaving surgery.* Crazy! I had them put me on a waiting list for an earlier slot; the scheduler, however, assured me that it would not happen because of scheduling difficulties and since it was the busy season—everyone wanted to get their procedures done before the end of the year for insurance purposes.

A couple of weeks later, John and I had our appointment with the plastic surgeon. Neither of us had ever been to a plastic surgeon before. It's like going to the doctor of the movie stars. First, you meet a 21-year-old Vanna White—a beautiful, young, perfectly made-up woman—and she asks you what kind of breasts you would like as she points to her own perfect breasts. Most of the surgeries are done to enhance outward appearances, and very few are for serious life-threatening things like cancer. It was surreal. At one point, they even took a picture of my breasts to put in a book.

Finally, we were going to meet the surgeon herself. She was running behind—still in surgery at the hospital—so we were sent home and told to come back at 6:00 p.m. after her surgery. When we arrived, she was noticeably exhausted but very professional. She told us that she considered herself an artist. I was just fine with that assessment since she was going to be the one in charge of my new breasts. She took us to her computer and showed us the different options of what women had done in breast reconstruction, but at one point, her computer took us to images of surgeries that had been botched—horrible pictures of distorted breasts. This was an accident, for which she profusely apologized, but John and I left very discouraged. God didn't allow me to stay down for long, though. John was so encouraging. "It's going to be fine," he said. "It'll all work out. I love you no matter what."

The next day, I was talking with my friend who told me, "Cindy, God is going to give you beautiful breasts." I thought, *Yes, that's who my God is, so I will believe it. I have an artist as a doctor; what more can I ask?* Spurgeon went on to say in that devotional, "He Who made no mistakes in balancing the clouds and meting out the Heavens, commits no errors in measuring out the ingredients which compose the medicine of souls."[10]

We came to an agreement on the size and type of breasts I should have. I wanted to go for the gusto, but later I got my ducks in a row and decided on a very average 34B. After all, walking down the halls with flashy DD cups could bring lots of whispering in the corners behind closed doors. Thank you, God, for sensible wisdom.

Then came the excruciating pain of a wait that was way too long. Patience is an attribute I have never possessed. During the wait, we took a superb trip to Kennebunkport, Maine, which we had previously scheduled with some dear friends.

"Cindy, this is just the thing we need to get our minds off the cancer stuff," John said. "We could think about the beach and yummy lobster rolls and New England clam chowder—they have the thick, creamy, chunky clam chowder with crusty bread. You love all of that."

"Yeah. That sounds fantastic. I'll get packing." The trip could be a recalibration—a reset back to focusing on living, not dying. Our friend Mike was fighting a recurrence of prostate cancer at the time, and I hoped we could mutually encourage each other. We stayed with Mike and Sally at their beach home.

The Bible says it's good to spend time with those who love God, for it brings true refreshment to our souls. "Perfume and incense bring joy to the heart, and the pleasantness of a friend springs from their heartfelt advice" (Prov. 27:9). We huddled in the living room between meals, pouring our hearts out to one another about God's

---

10. Ibid.

goodness in carrying us through the hardest difficulties of our lives. How good it was to be together that long weekend.

"I'm so happy we came, honey," I told John. "Thank you for the push."

"Well then, mission accomplished."

At the beach house, I was feeling a desperate need to get alone with God, my faithful, heavenly Father. I needed to hear from him and woke very early one morning to sit near the fireplace in a cozy, tailor-made chair just right for me, my coffee, and my Bible. I opened to the book of Job, a book I usually shy away from because of all Job's miseries, and settled on chapter 38. Oddly, it brought me so much comfort. This is what it says:

Then the Lord spoke to Job out of the storm. He said:

> *"Who is this that obscures my plans*
> *with words without knowledge?*
> *Brace yourself like a man;*
> *I will question you,*
> *and you shall answer me.*
>
> *"Where were you when I laid the earth's foundation?*
> *Tell me, if you understand.*
> *Who marked off its dimensions? Surely you know!*
> *Who stretched a measuring line across it?*
> *On what were its footings set,*
> *or who laid its cornerstone—*
> *while the morning stars sang together*
> *and all the angels shouted for joy?*
>
> *"Who shut up the sea behind doors*
> *when it burst forth from the womb,*
> *when I made the clouds its garment*
> *and wrapped it in thick darkness,*

when I fixed limits for it
   and set its doors and bars in place,
when I said, 'This far you may come and no farther;
   here is where your proud waves halt'?

"Have you ever given orders to the morning,
   or shown the dawn its place,
that it might take the earth by the edges
   and shake the wicked out of it?
The earth takes shape like clay under a seal;
   its features stand out like those of a garment."

—Job 38:1–14

Enough said, right? Yes, it seems harsh. "Where were you when I laid the earth's foundation?" (Job 38:4). We think we understand when we really have no inkling. "Who is this that obscures my plans with words without knowledge?" (Job 38:2). Obscure means not discovered or known about, uncertain. Yep, that's us. But it was comforting to me because God was telling me not to worry—he's got it covered. This much I'm sure of: God had arranged for me to read this chapter. He gave me the belief to know he was talking to me and giving me knowledge to know what he meant by those words. He who set the stars in the sky and tells the waves to halt would take care of me in my breast cancer. Every single molecule is in his capable care.

Romans sums up God's involvement in this disease when Paul says, "Oh, the depth of the riches of the wisdom and knowledge of God! How unsearchable his judgments, and his paths beyond tracing out!" (Rom. 11:33). No truer words were ever said. Breast cancer and goodness from God, I lack any glimmer of understanding. The chapter ends like this: "For from him and through him and for him are *all* things" (emphasis added) (Rom. 11:36).

Around that time, my close friends from Indianapolis decided they were going to pray for an earlier surgery appointment for me. I thanked them for the thought but assured them that it would never happen. I had been told by the staff that it was impossible. About three weeks later, I received a shocking call. An opening had come up, and in two days I would go in for surgery. The receptionist said this had never happened in the long history of their practice. *Wow! Only God.* My faith ballooned, rising high to the heavens. God catapulted me to certainty in him. *When will I ever learn not to limit God? Thank you, God, and thank you, friends, for believing God enough to pray.* I was thrilled. Finally, this disease was going to be eradicated. One thing about having cancer in your body is that you want it out ASAP. It's like having a sharp nail in you; just the thought is excruciating.

The night before the surgery, I had the shortest sleep in history. It was already 5:00 a.m., and I needed to get some cozy, comfy, trendy clothes on for my trip.

"Honey, what time exactly do we have to leave for the hospital?" John called from the bathroom.

"5:30."

"How are you feeling?"

"Amazingly well for the little sleep I had and this being the day they cut my breasts off."

"Cindy, don't be so dramatic."

"Well, that's what they're going to do."

"Yes, it's called a mastectomy."

"Got it. Remind me to call my dad on the way to let him know I'm okay."

I was feeling quite bright-eyed and bushy-tailed, stressfully excited, which was so weird for such a serious morning. Maybe the excitement was because the cancer was finally coming out.

In the car, I fumbled for my phone and pressed the numbers for dad.

"Hello?"

"Hi, Dad. I'm on the way to the hospital, feeling good about the surgery. I just wanted you to know I'm okay."

"I love you," he said. "Have John call us."

Conversations like this always went through Dad; Mom's stress level wouldn't handle them well. We arrived just in the nick of time, according to John. When we got into the hospital waiting area, we were greeted by no less than 30 of our friends to cheer us on. *Cheer* is kind of a strange word for an event where you get your breasts cut off—I mean, have a mastectomy. They were such terrific and hopeful support. We laughed and chatted until I had to go. Pastor Don said a prayer for me—a beautiful prayer. I know the Lord was pleased. Later, one of my friends said about that day, "Cindy, it was like you were going to a party instead of surgery." Again, God showed me his love through the special friends he had given me. Soon it would all be over. I'm undone sometimes as to how God brings me such wonderful care through his lovely people, now my cherished friends.

At the very beginning of all this, I made a commitment to the Lord that I was not going to think about the six-hour surgery or the fact that they were cutting my breasts off. Because of what I'd learned in his Word, I determined not to think on things that weren't true or excellent or hopeful or admirable. I determined to think about excellent, praiseworthy things. I had also learned to take thoughts captive and make them obedient to Christ (2 Cor. 10:5). It's a trust thing and a matter of keeping my mind on God.

Managing thoughts is possible only when we choose to see things from God's viewpoint. There's simply not any time to think about heartache and suffering when we're thinking lovely, admirable thoughts as the Lord directs us to do. Imagine how much lightheartedness we would have if we all did this. What if we accepted our day as from God the minute we woke up? How different would our lives be each day if we accepted with joy whatever the Lord brought? I know, it was profound for me, too—so profound that the dark morning of having my breasts removed felt like a party.

Let me give you another real-life example. When Adam got his driver's license, I had a talk with the Lord. I told him I was not going to give in to worry about his driving—not ever—because I'd seen all the lunatic helicopter moms, and I wasn't giving in to those contagious jitters. Adam got his license, and the commitment began. The first day, we got four inches of snow, and Adam had a 25-minute freeway drive to school. *Ha ha, Lord; very funny.* I got on my knees and said, *I'm not to worry or even think about this.* Every time my thoughts turned to driving, I'd stop and reaffirm my commitment. *God, you have to keep him safe anyway. I have no power. You have all the ability to protect him.* I had a wonderful experience with Adam driving. Why? Because I was not allowed to worry or fret over it, ever.

I put the truth on as they led me to surgery. *God has a good plan in all this, and he will bring just the right doctors and nurses and caregivers and therapy and medicines needed to help me. There's no need to stress one moment about it because it's quite easy to think myself into hysteria.* I can write a depressing novel in a nanosecond. How about you? What we put into our minds has a tremendous effect on what we think. Remember those scary movies we watched as a kid and then had nightmares? It didn't take long to realize that the way to avoid the nightmares was to stop watching the movies.

God has provided us with a way to overcome disparaging thoughts and behaviors and gain the self-control he wants for us. It's a matter of taking charge of thoughts and turning them into God's thoughts. Over every thought, I prayed, *Lord, help me every single time my mind goes to surgery and my breasts being cut off, which is often. I'm going to command myself not to think about it. Why? Because I'm going to show you, God, that I'm trusting you with my life and my breasts.*

I had two motives: to show God I believed him and to get that promised peace in Philippians 4:7. Earlier that surgery morning, I was nervous but not scared to death because I never allowed myself a single thought about what they were going to do to me that day—not one thought. I forced myself to think the right thoughts. The result was God's promised peace for being obedient. This was what God wanted me to do and what he helped me do.

We spend so much unprofitable time trying to figure out how to control our lives so we can have the outcomes we desire and hope for. Imagine if I had let my mind stray to my surgery; I would have wondered, *How am I going to feel after six long hours of being anesthetized? Probably nauseated and groggy, weak, not clear-headed.* I'd be thinking, *How much pain am I going to feel? My smiley face will maybe be an eight or nine. Will I wake up vomiting? I hate to throw up. I wonder how I will go to the bathroom. No, not a bed pan. What will my flat breasts look like?* Is there any benefit to this type of thinking? Would it have helped me solve my future? No. It would only be a hindrance to my peace, and it would keep me from trusting that God would take care of me, and his care is what I really needed.

The concept of controlling our thoughts doesn't just apply to cancer and surgery. Consider this. Earlier that summer, friends invited us to go whitewater rafting with our son—a last hurrah before college. I had never done that. It sounded fun, and I was excited to go. As I shared with others what I was about to do, I began hearing many tragic, scary stories. In one instance, a woman had fallen out of her raft, lodged her leg in the boulders under the rapids, and ended up with a broken leg. I sort of stopped listening when I heard that she fell out of the raft. Wait a minute! Do you mean to tell me you can fall out? I was also told that rafters wear helmets. Helmets to raft, really? What have I gotten myself into?

The night before the rafting excursion, I couldn't sleep a wink. I worried all night and had nightmares of falling out of the raft. The stories had lodged in my head, and I'd become very afraid. What a night that was! *I have to pull myself together. This is a special time for Adam—our last vacation before school starts*, I told myself. *What's true about rafting, and what am I wildly exaggerating? When I drive in my car, I put my seat belt on, but I don't go out thinking I'm going to have an accident, do I?* My straying thoughts had taken the fun out of this adventurous trip, and I had to back way up. *God, help me focus on the fun and not fear what will probably never happen.*

I had a fantastic trip and even rode in pole position on the raft. God knows what our minds need for peace and health and vitality. "The precepts of the LORD are right, giving joy to the heart. The commands of the LORD are radiant, giving light to the eyes" (Ps. 19:8).

Surgery went smoothly, just as anticipated. I woke from anesthesia very nauseated. John, who was able to stay with me in the hospital room this time, kept telling the nurses I was vomiting, so they kept coming in with those little Dramamine patches you wear for sea sickness. I had them all over my body. Finally, about midnight, the nauseated feeling stopped, and I was starving for some chicken soup. It's so good whenever you're sick, right? I only spent one night in the hospital. I was told my quick recovery was based on my lack of stress over the operation. Wow! Amazing! There really is something to listening to what God tells us about fixing our thoughts on the truth and not fabricating wild, worst-case scenarios of doom and gloom.

Over the next six months, I recuperated and went through the breast reconstruction process. Weekly, I went to the plastic surgeon's office, and she literally pumped my soon-to-be-breasts with saline as a way to stretch the skin for my 34B implants. I did my best to encourage my surgeon each week—after all, she was in charge of my new breasts. She was the one God had appointed to me. I would not use the word *vibrant* for her personality; she was more a matter-of-fact, stoic person. Always remembering that she considered herself an artist, each week I told her that she was going to give me beautiful breasts because she was an artist. I would repeat to her what my dear friend had told me about what God was going to give me.

It was a lengthy process, but after six months, the final surgery day came. I assured my plastic surgeon again that whatever she thought best in breast size and style was good. She was the artist. The surgery went according to plan. I was told that at one point the surgery team sat me up—in the middle of my procedure—and looked to see what size implant looked best for my body type. I must have given the surgeon confidence in her craft as an artist since she did consider giving me something other than a 34B.

When I woke up, I was completely bandaged around my chest like a mummy. I would have to wait three days before I could remove the dressing and see how my new breasts looked. I was so anxious to see how it all turned out. I could hardly wait. Finally, the third day came, and John helped me unveil. And there they were—not beautiful. They were horrific-looking breasts. I burst into tears. Poor John tried to console me the best he could. I'm sure he was shocked, too. I think we had both convinced ourselves that I was going to have beautiful, movie-star breasts. Regardless of what he thought, he said they were perfect, just what God had ordered. Well, that part was true. They were just what God ordered, except God's view of beautiful and my view were very different.

It took me a few days to come to grips with my new body and my disappointment, but then, as I thought about my situation—that I was alive and healthy and that God had gotten me through it—I felt more settled. God was bringing me comfort and factual truth about my circumstances. He was reminding me not to be overly concerned with what my body looked like on the outside but instead to really care about my heart and mind, the things that bring me the most happiness and life. God was revealing his perspective that I was alive and had survived breast cancer and was in really good physical health. Now that's wisdom from God.

Today, I love my breasts; they are so perfect for me. Only God could have given me the eyes and perspective to see things rightly through discouragement. There has not been one day in the last nine years that I have wished for my old breasts back. That's what God does for us when we turn our circumstances over to him and keep rightly focused. What he purposes is perfect for us. I'm so grateful for a husband who loves me so unwaveringly, so unconditionally, no matter what synthetic parts I have. He's 100 percent vested—all in—and fully supportive of me and our marriage. He truly loves me for who I am. *Thank you, God.*

CHAPTER SEVEN

The Rearview Mirror

Christian contentment is that sweet, inward,
quiet, gracious frame of spirit, which freely submits
to and delights in God's wise and fatherly
disposal in every condition.

—Jeremiah Burroughs

God was in the forefront all along, answering my begging heart for a really fun-in-the-sun memory with this lone kid of mine before college started in the fall. God didn't do what I wanted but what I *really* wanted. It wasn't my type of fun-and-games excitement, but it was a lasting, rich, memorable momentous time through breast cancer, a time in which we shared deeply personal things in our hearts—the important, meaningful, lasting stuff of life. Isn't this what every mom longs for? Adam's Christmas present to me that year was a framed picture of him sitting on my lap—now this boy of mine is a six-foot-tall man. The picture was full of meaning and quite endearing. Around the picture he wrote this:

Mom, your strength this year and faith that God would take care of us was amazing. That phone call at 7:30 when the nurse told you that you had cancer was the hardest thing I've ever had to hear. It makes me cry just to think about that night, just waiting for one simple call, just waiting and waiting, finally we get the call and wow that hurt. God has been so good to us through that trial. He has brought us so much closer and knit us together even more. Mom, your example is amazing. You have shown me the godly way of dealing with hardship and disease. Mom, you are such a gift to me and the thought of losing you was heart-wrenching. It was so hard, and God made it so good.

I love you so much,
Adam

The gift every mom longs for, right? I just imagine the strength Adam has accumulated through this painful process. The Bible says that suffering produces perseverance, perseverance produces character, and produces hope (Rom. 5:3–5). James 1:2 tells us that we should consider it pure joy whenever we face trials of many kinds because it produces perseverance. There's that word again. As Adam's mom, every molecule in my being hungers for him to be the leader God desires for him to be, because I know that what he's learned will get him through all sorts of suffering in this life. I must admit, though, that it's heart-wrenching to watch him struggle with even the slightest difficulty.

I have been thinking about how Adam has experienced God's personal care and love through that most painful season of his young life. Think about the foundation he will have when turmoil comes his way. That alone makes cancer worth it to me. My dear friend Susie, who later died of breast cancer, shared with me at her kitchen table, through many tears, that if her only daughter—10 years old at the time—would grow to be close to God through her cancer, it would be worth it. We realized when the rubber hits the road and everything is stripped away, laid bare, that what her daughter and my son needed more than even their moms was our heavenly Father holding them in his mighty, strong arms under his magnificent care. That's what they need the most. That is the full truth whether we believe it or not. Our help comes from the Lord, "the Maker of heaven and earth" (Ps. 121:2).

Years ago, I had the privilege of meeting John Piper—a true honor for me as I have followed his teaching for years. The way he digs into the Word of God and brings it to life—real, life-giving life—resonates with my own relationship with Jesus. He's the real deal when it comes to people who love Jesus and his truth. He's a gifted teacher of the Bible and brings it to his listeners in a hopeful, helpful, inspiring way. He has a way of building you up as if you just received an inoculation of super-vitamins to any part of your weakened heart. The day I met him, I heard him speak on God's sovereignty, even in death. I had always known God was involved in Jonathan's death; I knew it in my bones, but I was younger in my faith and didn't know all the scriptures as well as Piper did. Any time I shared that God was involved in Jonathan's death, I got shot down. Not knowing the scriptures kept me feeling uncertain, so I stayed quiet. What did I know, anyway? But in my heart, I knew that God was there all along, orchestrating every detail of Jonathan's existence. Some tried to tell me that God would never cause death, but I knew enough of the Bible to know that wasn't true. Think of Noah and the flood God brought. God had a purpose for Jonathan's life and death, just as he does for my own life and death—and yours, too. Look at what he says in Isaiah 45:7: "I form the light and create darkness, I bring prosperity and create disaster; I, the LORD do all these things." And 1 Samuel 2:6 says, "The LORD brings death and makes alive; he brings down to the grave and raises up." Another one that I cling to is Deuteronomy 32:39: "See now that I myself am he! There is no god besides me. I put to death and I bring to life, I have wounded and I will heal, and no one can deliver out of my hand."

What I didn't understand was how people could think any less of God than exactly who he is as explained in his Word—the Creator who has absolute power over everything. Would we want a lesser God, one we completely understand? Seems like we want God to exceed our knowledge and be beyond our understanding. Job 36:26 says, "How great is God—beyond our understanding!" God is just that powerful. It can be a difficult thing to wrap our minds around the fact that God brings death, but he who knows and sees the future not only knows the outcome of that future but is the architect and builder of it. He controls all the details of it all the way to eternity. Our God loved his created people so much that he sent his Son, Jesus, to die on that appalling cross so we could have a relationship with him and be with him forever in heaven. When I plunged in and got to know him, before my eyes he began revealing things to me in his Word. If I kept reading, studying, seeking, and believing what he was saying in the scriptures, I could then understand him. How can I deny all those verses that speak right to my soul?

When Piper talked about God's involvement in a person's death, it spoke right to my heart. I wanted to jump out of my chair. Finally, someone who knows. Ever felt that way? Something you've known to be right or true all along finally bursts with light, shining right into your soul. It brought the much-needed affirmation of God and a confidence in his love and supreme control over all things. I rest just knowing that he has power even over death and that I don't need to be in that driver's seat.

That day I heard Piper speak, I made my way up through the people, determined to talk with him. I saw a crack and weaseled my way in.

"Pastor Piper, my name is Cindy. It's a pleasure to meet you," I said. "I've been following your teaching for years. Thank you for your commitment to God and his Word." I really meant it. "I have a promise to make to you."

"A promise?"

"Yes. I've always known that God is supreme over life and death and that he is the planner of our lives. My son passed away at five days."

"I'm sorry to hear that."

"Pastor Piper, God took my son. I've always known and have great comfort and much hope over that fact. Thank you for showing me so much more of God through your teaching on what exactly it says in his Word on this subject."

"You're welcome, Cindy. What's the promise?"

"I promise I will never again say God allowed my son's death. No, no, I will say God brought Jonathan's death, just like he brought his life, for plans and purposes only he fully knows. It seems anything less would belittle God by depicting him as not supreme in Jonathan's short life on earth."

The solid, concrete truth is that he has supreme control over every matter in heaven, on the earth, and under the earth. Revelation 4:11 says, "For you created all things, and by your will they were created and have their being." Romans 11:36 says, "From him and through him and for him are all things."

Look at what happened to Lazarus in the Bible. He was sick and living in the village of Bethany with his sisters, Mary and Martha. The sisters sent word to Jesus, "'Lord, the one you love is sick.' When he heard this, Jesus said, 'This sickness will not end in death. No, it is for God's glory so that God's Son may be glorified through it'" (John 11:3–4). God had a specific purpose for Lazarus's deadly illness, and interestingly, we are told that it was for God's glory. Odd, don't you think? How could God be honored and revered as great and majestic in a severely ill man? Lazarus ends up dying. Jesus had just said his sickness would not end in death, but it did. In the same way, I have to trust God even when it doesn't make any sense at all. Worse than that, when it looks dreadfully awful, I have to realize that God is at work doing something good because that's who he is—all good in cancer, in Jonathan's death, and even cancer again.

Jesus didn't come to save Lazarus but to let him die. Mary and Martha were devastated. They had called for Jesus to come and heal this poor man, but Jesus had let him die to bring God glory. Seems crazy. Why, God? Lazarus had been dead for four days before Jesus came to see him. Then Jesus said, "Lazarus is dead, and for your sake I am glad I was not there, so that you may believe" (John 11:14–15). He sounded so harsh and illogical, yet Jesus wept when he saw Mary and the others weeping over Lazarus's death, and he asked the people to take him to Lazarus's tomb. Note that Jesus was devastated over the death, yet he did not prevent it. I bet Jesus was weeping when he took Jonathan home, too.

When they arrived at Lazarus's tomb, Jesus told them to remove the stone. Martha warned him that there'd be a bad odor since Lazarus had been dead for four days. But Jesus replied, "Did I not tell you that if you believe, you will see the glory of God?" (John 11:40). Well, yes, he had said that. Jesus looked up and, praying to God the Father in heaven, said, "Father, I thank you that you have heard me. I knew that you always hear me, but I said this for the benefit of the people standing here, that they may believe that you sent me" (John 11:41–42). He was revealing the purposes behind Lazarus's death, and one purpose was so the people would believe.

Then, in a loud voice, Jesus commanded Lazarus to come out of the tomb. "The dead man came out, his hands and feet wrapped with strips of linen, and a cloth around his face" (John 11:44). Jesus's plan all along was to raise Lazarus from the dead. Wow! That answers a lot of the why questions: why he let him die, why he was glad he died, why it was good for us to experience this, and why he was going to get honor and greatness and majesty from this. Jesus had said, "This sickness will not end in death" (John 11:4), yet human eyes had seen death. Only Jesus saw God working his master plan—

the perfect, good, best plan for all. The ultimate end of Lazarus's sickness was restrained. There was a limit beyond which it could not go. All our sicknesses have their limits; all our pain has its limits; all our trials have their limits. If it is not in God's good, perfect plan for us to experience something, we will not experience it. That's a lesson worth knowing.

At church recently, our pastor read from Exodus 14, and I learned yet again how God's plans reach far beyond the limits of what I can see. This passage shows us how the Lord had Moses bring the Israelites on a roundabout way to the Red Sea so Pharaoh, who was pursuing them with the intent to kill them, would catch them. Did you hear that? So Pharaoh would catch them. The Lord said, "I will harden Pharaoh's heart, and he will pursue them" (Exod. 14:4). What? Harden a man's heart so he will want to kill? What, God, are you doing? It sounds like a trap, right? In a way, it was, but God said, "I will gain glory for myself through Pharaoh and all his army, and the Egyptians will know that I am the LORD" (Exod. 14:4). The Lord took the Israelites right to the dead end, to the point of capture, to the banks of the Red Sea, which would give them no way out. At that point, I'm thinking how that would devastate me. But God told Moses to raise his staff over the Red Sea, and the water literally parted from a wind so strong that it made the ground dry, letting the Israelites walk right though the sea to the other side. The Egyptians were not so lucky. After they had passed through the water, the Lord told Moses to hold his staff up again, and the water flowed over all the Egyptians.

Sometimes our lives look so impossible, like a complete, colossal disaster, the deadest end. That's when God asks us to traverse the mountain with faith (mustard-seed faith), bravery, and belief that God will deliver us all the way to the other side. This mustard-seed faith is supernatural, from God. "If you have faith as small as a mustard seed, you can say to this mountain, 'Move from here to there,' and it will move. Nothing will be impossible for you" (Matt.

17:20). When it seems hopelessly absurd, put your biggest-girl pants on because God's coming to deliver you. Psalm 34:17 says he hears and delivers us from all our troubles. He is doing his work every moment with every molecule of our lives, even when we don't see it. His safekeeping is sure and certain, free from fault or crack, a complete fortress, a citadel like no other. I'm sure Moses was terrified and the Israelites were afraid, yet God was fighting for them. He's fighting for you and me, too. When the Israelites saw God rescuing them, they "put their trust in him and in Moses his servant" (Exod. 14:31). God's purposes for my life and yours are profoundly bigger than what we see. I'm learning to keep trusting in his outcome. It's much more enormous than anything I could put together.

I'm learning to cope with my own troubles from these examples of struggling people in the Bible. God wrote his book especially for us to know him, his ways, and how he works in people's lives. This is so valuable that I want to understand all of it.

The Bible tells us that King Nebuchadnezzar ordered everyone to bow down to him and worship a golden image of himself. Three men—Shadrach, Meshach, and Abednego, who were followers of God—refused. Though the men knew that the penalty for their refusal was death by being thrown into the king's fiery furnace, they still chose certain death over worshiping anyone other than the one true God. They trusted God so much and were so devoted to living for him that they were willing to be burned up in a furnace rather than worship someone else. Wow! I have a lot to learn—or, I should say, *believe*.

When an official came to Nebuchadnezzar and told him about Shadrach, Meshach, and Abednego, the king was infuriated. He had the furnace turned up seven times hotter and had the men bound with all their clothes on and thrown into the furnace—a furnace so hot that the king's officials died when they threw the three men into the fire. Shadrach, Meshach, and Abednego should have died instantly, but instead, something amazing happened.

Then King Nebuchadnezzar leaped to his feet in amazement and asked his advisers, "Weren't there three men that we tied up and threw into the fire?"

They replied, "Certainly, Your Majesty."

He said, "Look! I see four men walking around in the fire, unbound and unharmed, and the fourth looks like a son of the gods."

—Dan. 3:24–25

This is for you and me—written down so we would *believe* how much he loves us. God cares no less for me than he does for those men in the furnace. He wants me to believe this and for you to believe it, also.

Nebuchadnezzar then approached the opening of the blazing furnace and shouted, "Shadrach, Meshach and Abednego, servants of the Most High God, come out! Come here!"

—Dan. 3:26

Nebuchadnezzar's eyes were suddenly opened, and he saw that God was real. When the three faithful men came out of the fire, those near them saw that "the fire had not harmed their bodies, nor was a hair of their heads singed; their robes were not scorched, and there was no smell of fire on them" (Dan. 3:27). What a site that must have been!

Then Nebuchadnezzar said, "Praise be to the God of Shadrach, Meshach and Abednego, who has sent his angel and rescued his servants! They trusted in him and defied the king's command and were willing to give up their lives rather than serve or worship any god except their own God."

—Dan. 3:28

What an amazing legacy these men left and what influence the experience must have had on those who witnessed it. I imagine these guys were totally calm and confident, knowing beyond a shadow of doubt that God would take care of them, whatever the outcome.

I want to be like Shadrach, Meshach, and Abednego and live with the same sold-out confidence in God's care for me. Through each adversity, I gain a little more trust, a little more belief in my completely trustworthy God. Even in modern times through biographies and documentaries, we can learn from soldiers and prisoners of war who trusted God through extreme circumstances. God is still involved today, telling us that not a hair on our heads will be touched without his allowing it because he is covering and controlling our situations. He's supreme.

> *When you pass through the waters,*
> *I will be with you;*
> *and when you pass through the rivers,*
> *they will not sweep over you.*
> *When you walk through the fire,*
> *you will not be burned;*
> *the flames will not set you ablaze.*
>
> —Isa. 43:2

Only the Lord knows our greatest needs through times of difficulties and suffering. If the furnace is being turned up, there's a good reason.

When frightening situations come our way, we can take courage knowing that our hardships have mighty purposes—God's purposes. He says there's joy in our trials because he's working them for much good, and the testing of our faith produces perseverance. There's that word again. *Perseverance* is a word we don't hear much nowadays. It means we strain and strive to get something more from our struggle. To persevere means to persist, continue, carry on, keep going, struggle on, hammer away, stand fast, hold on, go the distance, stop at nothing, leave no stone unturned. Charles Spurgeon puts it beautifully.

> The limitation [of our pain] is tenderly set. The knife of the heavenly Surgeon never cuts deeper than is absolutely necessary. "He doth not afflict willingly nor grieve the children of men" (Lam. 3:33). A mother's heart cries, "Spare my child!" but no mother is more compassionate than our gracious God. When we consider how obstinate we are, it is a wonder that we are not driven with a sharper bit. It is very comforting to know that He who has set the boundaries of our habitation has also set the boundaries of our tribulation.[11]

The Job passage I read in Kennebunkport while waiting for my mastectomy also meant a lot to me because it's true. Where were you when I (God) was creating planet Earth? Where were you when I was marking the boundaries?

Knowing all this, we must follow day by day in full trust, not trying to determine or manipulate what the outcome of a particular situation will be but focusing on what God is doing. Matthew 6:34 says, "Therefore do not worry about tomorrow, for tomorrow will worry about itself. Each day has enough trouble of its own." The outcome of our circumstances is God's alone. The book of our life is already finished, and we win both now on earth and whenever God decides to take us home to him. What matters most is whether I am following, experiencing, believing, and walking in what Jesus is asking of me today. Jesus, my pilot, is with me all the way to the other side—heaven—as he has promised. Isaiah 41:13 says, "For I am the LORD your God who takes hold of your right hand and says to you, Do not fear; I will help you."

---

11. Ibid.

Every morning I get up and spend my first moments, about one hour, with the Lord. It's my favorite time of day because I spend that time looking at the things he has to say, things like he will never forget me. He is right next to me. He is holding me in his strong, mighty arms.

> *Can a mother forget the baby at her breast*
>   *and have no compassion on the child she has borne?*
> *Though she may forget,*
>   *I will not forget you!*
> *See, I have engraved you on the palms of my hands;*
>   *your walls are ever before me.*
>   —Isa. 49:15–16

Who wouldn't want that every day? Because the Lord is laying out my day and putting thoughts of perfect peace in my mind, I can't spend time worrying about the future of my day. That's how he works; he gives us what we need for what's directly in front of us—not years, months, weeks, or even sometimes days ahead. Each morning he gives me comfort, council, help, hope, strength, encouragement, and a good attitude, which I absolutely need every day.

For example, one morning recently, I woke with such a heavy heart for John. He was struggling in a very new field of work in which he was working with many lawyers, though he was not a lawyer, negotiating contracts. Every word counts in a contract. My heart was so heavy for him. My heart also ached for some friends who were struggling with health issues. So I opened my Bible and asked the Lord for encouragement. I read until I heard God speak into my situation. When I got to a passage in Mark, there it was:

> *"Have faith in God," Jesus answered. "Truly I tell you, if anyone says to this mountain, 'Go, throw yourself into the sea,' and does not doubt in their heart but believes that what they say will happen, it will be done for them. Therefore I*

*tell you, whatever you ask for in prayer, believe that you
have received it, and it will be yours. And when you stand
praying, if you hold anything against anyone, forgive them,
so that your Father in heaven may forgive you your sins."*

—Mark 11:22–26

What a comfort! God was answering my heart's cries right then. *Thank you, Jesus!* Now I must put that on and live in that helpful, hopeful encouragement. *Help me do it, God.*

Last year, I ran into an acquaintance at the post office, and she told me that she'd had breast cancer 10 years ago. I asked how she was doing, and she replied, "Not well." Her "not well" seemed like a response to the fact that she'd had breast cancer—10 years ago. Even though she was in remission, had a good prognosis, and was in great health, her view was "not well." I empathized with her pain because that was me a few years ago. Just like her, I, too, wanted to wear the cancer mantel. If we let it, cancer has a way of defining who we are in the present rather than remaining something we had been through in the past. I've seen this mentality quite often. I know it well in my own life. It's a poisonous reel of bad tape in our minds that can paralyze and depress even the most vibrant people. I can sniff it out a mile away. We are to look forward, not backward. "Brothers and sisters, I do not consider myself yet to have taken hold of it. But one thing I do; Forgetting what is behind and straining toward what is ahead" (Phil. 3:13).

It's so easy to focus on how sorry we feel for ourselves. Believe me, this is close up and personal for me. We all do it to one degree or another. I call it the poor-me tape we play in our heads over and over. It begins to define us, and we render ourselves unable to move on to the real life going on right in front of us. Self-pity cripples and paralyzes us from the delightful, joyful abundant life God planned. In John 10:10, Jesus says, "The thief [Satan] comes only to steal and kill and destroy; I have come that they may have life, and have it to the full." But rather than accept that abundant life, we tend to walk the I'm-the-only-one-dealing-with-hard-things road—and that's a horrible place to be. There's just no truth there. Our antidote is to be thankful in all circumstances. Why? This is God's will for you (1 Thess. 5:18). God wants us believing and trusting and living, not looking backward. Let us learn to press forward, living life even when it's legitimately hard. He's a promise-keeping, way-making, covenant-keeping God who knows every hair on our heads. "Indeed, the very hairs of your head are all numbered. Don't be afraid; you are worth more than many sparrows" (Luke 12:7). Let's let go of our past hardships and move on to living the vibrant life of John 10:10.

Today, I'm like a blind woman feeling her way home. I'm finding these precepts God gives are so much more than good ideas; they are my life preservers, my heavenly flotation devices. "Your statutes are my delight; they are my counselors. Cause me to understand the way of your precepts, that I may meditate on your wonderful deeds" (Ps. 119:24, 27). Christians can still get stuck in the mud up to their knees in a lost cause every now and then. I'm always looking back to what just happened to me as I step deep in the quicksand of circumstances. Then the revelation comes: I'm in weeds, deep in the woods, with no ducks in my row. That human frailty of faulty thinking is why we need each other to remind us of the way. It takes a village of God's Word, godly friends, mentors, pastors, and time for our wandering hearts to come around to the truth of our situations.

Last night I watched a TV series called *The Good Place*. It portrayed heaven as a place where you can get in if you're good. It portrayed God as someone who needs our help to figure things out. Think about how silly that is—that our God who made us and the 100 billion galaxies in the observable universe would need our help to figure out anything. That's how we tend to approach him, though, isn't it? Sometimes I tell God how things should be—like

God needs my help. I think I have a stake in the situation, but that is so untrue. He is the one who says something like this to you:

> Do not lift your hand to attempt to accomplish any slightest task in your own strength.
> This I have forbidden. . . .
> And if I bring you through the river in summer,
> you shall not fear to trust Me in the flood time.
> So clasp your hand in Mine, and do not loosen your hold.
> For you cannot tell what great thing I may do for you through some small happening.
> Your every hair is numbered. . . .
> Look not back, but look ahead,
> for I have glory prepared for you.[12]

God wants to give us his peace, "which transcends all understanding" (Phil. 4:7). We don't have to live in fear—especially the fear of failing health. You could be saying, "Easier said than done." Agreed! Just yesterday I heard of two people who are struggling with debilitating fear, so much so that one of them went to therapy for it—understandably. If we let that torturer in, it will control us to the point that we will need medical and emotional help to function. Having said that, I'm grateful we have bridges to get us through when our faith is crashing. You may know someone struggling with this fear, or you could be struggling. If fear has overtaken your life or the life of someone you love, find help. Find a friend who will pray for you, who will help you get that beast back in its cage. God reminds us in 2 Timothy 1:7 that God has not given us a spirit of fear, but of power, love, and self-discipline. Fear begins in our minds—minds that have been allowed to wander and make unrealistic allusions and

---

12. Francis J. Roberts, "Do Not Look Back," *Come Away My Beloved . . . And Pray*, Google Books.

faulty assumptions. That's why it's so important to take our thoughts captive and put on true, lovely, praiseworthy thoughts as God tells us to (Phil. 4:8). It's a necessity for a peaceful, sound mind.

I use this as my filter for every single struggle I encounter:

God's Filter of Life

1. Put God in the center of your circumstance: "Give thanks in all circumstances; for this is God's will for you in Christ Jesus" (1 Thess. 5:18).
2. Tell yourself the truth that God has good in this: "And we know that in all things God works for the good of those who love him, who have been called according to his purpose" (Rom. 8:28).
3. Remind yourself that you are to trust God with this, no matter what it is: "Trust in the LORD with all of your heart and lean not on your own understanding; in all your ways submit to him, and he will make your paths straight" (Prov. 3:5–6).
4. Stop thinking you can fix it, control it, or know better than God does about it: "Do not be wise in your own eyes" (Prov. 3:7). His ways are better than your ways, because his ways are heavenly (Isa. 55:8–11).

I recommend writing these on a card to take everywhere with you. It will be a lifeline when needed—not just for you but for all those God intersects in your life.

Recently, I took a walk with a friend whose husband is in home hospice with stage IV liver cancer and whose 20-something-year-old son is living at home with severe Crohn's disease. Her son is down to 108 pounds, yet she told me, "The good news is his blood work is normal." She is rejoicing for that today. I'm watching God sustain her every day as she turns her eyes to God for help, as she looks ahead and lives in this present day today—not allowing herself to step into the quicksand of despair, that hopeless spiral down. I admit, it's very hard for me to keep from asking about her thoughts about the future—I want to help her plan. I want to help get her settled after her horrific fate ends. But I can see that God is taking care of each step while she so tenderly, so lovingly cares for the two most important people in her life. I've realized that God gives us capacity when we need it. Too much capacity, and we are undone, paralyzed. My friend only has capacity to care for her family today. God will do tomorrow. Do not worry about your needs; your heavenly Father knows you need them (Matt. 6:25–34). Do the work in front of you, the one you're called to do, and as you do, these needs will be given to you. My friend is exactly in the right spot. I'm so glad God showed me so I wouldn't get her off track, the good track she's on, all her ducks in a row. *Thank you, God.*

As we turn our heads upward to God, who is in the center of our lives, trusting his good plan in our suffering, he promises to carry us all the way to the other side, our home. At the end of a long day, Jesus said to his disciples:

> *"Let us go over to the other side." Leaving the crowd behind, they took him along, just as he was, in the boat. There were also other boats with him. A furious squall came up, and the waves broke over the boat, so that it was nearly swamped. Jesus was in the stern, sleeping on a cushion. The disciples woke him and said to him, "Teacher, don't you care if we drown?"*
>
> *He got up, rebuked the wind and said to the waves, "Quiet! Be still!" Then the wind died down and it was completely calm.*
>
> *He said to his disciples, "Why are you so afraid? Do you still have no faith?"*
>
> *They were terrified and asked each other, "Who is this? Even the wind and the waves obey him!"*
>
> —Mark 4:35–41

The disciples were terrified. I'd be terrified. They were caught in a horrible storm and sinking, but Jesus was sleeping on a cushion in the back of the boat—sleeping. To me, it sounds legitimate to be scared to death and wake Jesus; after all, they had seen him perform miracles. They knew he was the Son of the Most High God, and they knew he had power. Why wouldn't they wake him? The waves were crashing over the boat—they were sinking. Jesus, however, rebuked the disciples for their lack of faith when they woke him. Sounds kind of harsh, don't you think? But it actually makes sense when you look closer—and because Jesus is always right. Look at what Jesus said in the first sentence: "Let us go over to the other side of the lake." If Jesus—God in human flesh—tells you that you are going to the other side of the lake, you are going to the other side of the lake. It's an absolute, 100-percent fact. If Jesus says so, it is so.

I'm just like those disciples. Even though God has said he is caring for me and carrying me in his hands, I get afraid and forget what he has said. You see why I love these stories? I see myself in them. They build my faith in God's care for me and remind me that he is with me even when I'm having trouble fully believing.

When I remind myself that God is holding me, I put on what is called the four *F*s. Then I am able to move from panic to peacefulness right in the midst of completely overwhelming circumstances.

1. What are the *facts* about my situation?
2. What does *faith* say about those facts?
3. I should *function* based on that information.
4. My *feelings* then fall peacefully into place because I have put them where they belong, at the caboose.

The other day, I received a text from one of my bff's Carrie. Her doctor had found a mass on her 30-something-year-old daughter Amber's ovary, and her tumor markers were very high. This was very concerning news. Amber had two young children and another child a bit older. Amber called me in hysterics, as you can imagine. She was sure she had cancer and was going to die. We prayed to the only one who has the power over this situation, the Maker of heaven and earth, where our help comes from (Ps. 121:2).

If you get a call like this, always pray with the person—awkward or not, just pray.

I knew her naturally wild, straying mind well. I'd lived in that mind. I've been that mind. The four *F*s came to my thoughts: What were the facts of her situation? She had high tumor markers and a mass. What did faith say about this tumor? God was in the center of her circumstances and had her covered. Following our time of prayer, she calmed right down, and God got those wild feelings back where they belonged—in the caboose of her brain. She later said how peaceful and lighthearted she became. *Thank you, God!* Our part in gaining the peace and comfort God offers is simply to put his truth in the center of the situation and then rest and wait as you pray patiently. The result is all up to him.

Consider another dear friend of mine Michelle, who was dying of liver cancer. One day as she was reading her Bible, she came across this passage: "Have I not commanded you? Be strong and courageous. Do not be afraid; do not be discouraged, for the LORD your God will be with you wherever you go" (Josh. 1:9). Michelle had three young children. Not wanting her family to hurt when she died, she began to distance herself from them, thinking distance would protect them from the pain of her death. As a mom, I could totally understand her reasoning, as I'm sure you can. But God intervened and helped Michelle see how important it was for the family to have the opportunity to take care of her. God brought her help and peace as she allowed them to love on her in the way she so needed—and that they needed to give her. She clung to the words God gave her in Joshua 1:9 and quoted them to me often during her suffering. Those divinely given words she stored in the forefront of her mind. When God gives you a scripture in your darkest moment, it becomes your pacifier of hope. Nothing satisfies your ache more. To me, her story was a complete picture of controlling the mind to what God wants in it to bring about his supernatural peace. It can be so difficult but so worth it. There's nothing like God's care in tragedies. The Apostle Paul also had to learn contentment:

> *I have learned to be content whatever the circumstances. I know what it is to be in need, and I know what it is to have plenty. I have learned the secret of being content in any and every situation, whether well fed or hungry, whether living in plenty or in want. I can do all this through him who gives me strength.*
>
> —Phil. 4:11–13

Now let me remind you, Paul was imprisoned, flogged, shipwrecked, and tortured. The list is extensive. When he talks about learning contentment, well, it's radical (2 Cor. 11:16–33).

Imagine putting that faith on. I'm sure he worked hard as nails to see God's love for him in the middle of being flogged. The Bible says these men are just like us. My friend Michelle had heard from God, but she had to remind herself of what he said moment by moment, day by day to receive comfort from it. I have found that when God speaks to us, he asks us to put on the words and promises that he's given us. Michelle needed to hear from God and know he was near, that he was going to get her through to the other side.

Like Michelle, we need to hear from God to know that he's going to get us through to the other side. The other day, I went to the beach with a group of new friends who'd recently moved to Florida. It was a picture-perfect day. The winds were calm with a gentle breeze on our backs, just enough to keep us cool. The sun was in all its glory, and we all lathered up for our time in the rays. Judy—we call her Mary Poppins because she has every tchotchke for the beach you could ever want—was putting up the umbrellas and getting the huge floats ready for the 88-degree water. As I sat on the beach next to one friend, a door opened for me to share. It was one of those moments when the light bulb goes on, and I knew it was time to speak about God's goodness in my life. Of course, that included the story of my cancer. I began sharing how good God had been to me in my difficulties, and then my friend sharply interrupted, "If that happened to me, I would curse God."

"What?" I was stunned. I had no box in my brain for that perspective. Wow! All I had been through evoked disgust in her, while for me it was an amazing reminder of my abundant supply of hope and care from my heavenly Father. As I tried hard to wrap my arms around this news, I said, "I can see that if you don't have God in your life, if you have no place for him, you might feel like cursing him." It was hard even to get those words out because they are so contrary, so antagonistic to who God is and what is true. *Oh, Lord, please help her.* At that moment I realized that without God in our lives, we feel we must control and fix and be supreme over all our tragedies. What a hopeless, slippery slide of discouragement, depression, anxiety, and fear. Satan is the father of all lies. Believing that God is not good means we are believing one of Satan's fiercest lies. John 10:10 says the thief (Satan) comes to kill, steal, and destroy, bringing darkness over our lives.

I gave a talk a few years ago called "From the Grave to the Banquet Hall." I think that visual is a good picture. I asked a group of women to make a beautiful banquet table that sparkled as if a celebrity were invited. They went all out with candelabras, gold trimmings, crystal—it was gorgeous. I then had another group make a table with the grossest things they could find. They also went all out—a little too far out, taking a baby's diaper and adding melted chocolate. The point was stark and vividly clear. When we don't have God in our lives, we are playing in dirty, filthy mud pies of unbelief when a holiday at the sea awaits us.

It doesn't make sense until we begin to see from God's point of view, from his divine perspective, from clear lenses versus our defective ones. There's a Chinese parable that goes like this:

> A farmer and his son had a beloved stallion that helped the family earn a living. One day, the horse ran away and their neighbors exclaimed, "Your horse ran away, what terrible luck!" The farmer replied, "Maybe yes, maybe no. We'll see."
>
> A few days later, the horse returned home, leading a few wild mares back to the farm as well. The neighbors shouted out, "Your horse has returned, and brought several horses home with him. What great luck!" The farmer replied, "Maybe yes, maybe no. We'll see."
>
> Later that week, the farmer's son was trying to break one of the mares and she threw him to the ground, breaking his leg. The villagers cried, "Your son broke his leg, what terrible luck!" The farmer replied, "Maybe yes, maybe no. We'll see."
>
> A few weeks later, soldiers from the national army marched through town, conscripting all the able-bodied boys for the army. They did not take the farmer's son because of his injury. Friends shouted, "Your boy is spared, what incredible luck!" To which the farmer replied, "Maybe yes, maybe no. We'll see."[13]

The point for us Christians is that God has the only true, right, pure perspective. If he says it's important to give thanks, then give thanks, knowing it's the very best thing for you to do. Of course, my

---

13. Cardwell C. Nuckols, PhD, *Finding Freedom through Illumination: Achieving Christ-Consciousness* (Deerfield Beach, FL: Health Communications, Inc., 2014), 154–156.

friend wondered how I could be grateful and see anything positive in cancer. I get it. It was so hard for me until God began to give me the eyes to see. Now I look for him, for his fingerprints as someone searching for pure gold. Why? Because it's a treasure worth finding, and he's a treasure worth knowing. Matthew 13:44 says that the kingdom of heaven is like a treasure hidden in a field. When you find it, you will sell everything you own to buy that field.

Later, my friend was diagnosed with a dreadful disease. She had a difficult, roller-coaster ride but has shared how she might become more interested in God. Why? Could it be because she's seeing him in her care? He's making himself known to her as he did for me during my Hodgkin's disease. How exciting to see God at work on my friend's behalf.

My sufferings were absolutely necessary and the most loving thing God could have given me because they brought me to him so I could see him, know him, and experience him and his highest best.

"A rising tide lifts all the boats,"[14] John F. Kennedy once said. I'm a boat lifting on a rising tide to the high seas with Captain Jesus at my helm. Hodgkin's disease brought me that real relationship I was missing in my life. God brought me my greatest treasure—Jesus— the one who cares, comforts, strengthens, equips, helps, and listens. He's the supreme one who's directing today's details, and he will direct my homecoming to heaven at exactly his appointed time, only after my fully planned life on earth. Oh, how great that will be!

Just this morning I read, "Those who look to him are radiant; their faces are never covered with shame" (Ps. 34:5). After so many years of walking with Jesus—sometimes being carried by him—I love this verse because it reminds me that Jesus is near to me 100

---

14. John F. Kennedy, "Remarks in Heber Springs, Arkansas, at the Dedication of Greers Ferry Dam," *The American Presidency Project*, https://www.presidency.ucsb.edu/documents/remarks-heber-springs-arkansas-the-dedication-greers-ferry-dam.

percent of my day. I don't have a care or worry that he's not conscious of and concerned about. Most importantly, he's working everything out to the best end. With Jesus, I will never be left wanting. He's right next to me. "Those who look to him are radiant." The word *radiant* means sending out light, shining or glowing brightly. Some of its synonyms are *shining, bright, illuminated, brilliant, gleaming,* and *ablaze.* Since my name, Cindy, actually means radiant one, this word from God for me has extra special meaning. I'm the very best version of myself, of Cindy, radiant, when I keep my eyes fixed on God. How personal! And this is just one single day of spending time with Jesus. Think of all that 33 years have brought.

Jesus makes life exciting and thrilling and happy and content and joyful and peaceful. Although my trials have been very painful, I now know God always has a purpose for me in them—a supreme purpose. I can't always understand it or see it, but I can surely ask for trust. I can say he will make it all good at the right time, and I ask him to show me and help, help, help me persevere and endure until it comes to pass. I open his Word—his love letter, as it has been called—and let him speak to me. My situation may be dark, scary, and painful, but with God at the helm, how could I not say that all will be well?

> *You make known to me the path of life;*
> *you will fill me with joy in your presence,*
> *with eternal pleasures at your right hand.*
>
> —Ps. 16:11

Sometimes God heals, and it's unbelievably wonderful. Sometimes he puts us in the fiery furnace for a season. In both situations, he is delivering us, speaking to us, and revealing himself and his kindness. I'd like to say he heals just like we want him to, but then it wouldn't be our best. We want his supremely great outcome.

Grab hold. The best is yet to come.

> *May the God of hope fill you with all joy and peace as you trust in him, so that you may overflow with hope by the power of the Holy Spirit.*
>
> —Rom. 15:13